Learn How to Draw

Create Your Own Amazing Shapes and Figures (Doodle and Zen, Drawing People)

By Lucy Warner

Table of Contents

Learn How to Draw

Create Your Own Amazing Shapes and Figures (Doodle and Zen, Drawing People)

Disclaimer

While all attempts have been made to verify the information provided in this book, the author does not assume any responsibility for errors, omissions, or contrary interpretations of the subject matter contained within. **The information provided in this book is for educational and entertainment purposes only. The reader is responsible for his or her own actions, and the author does not accept any responsibilities for any liabilities or damages, real or perceived, resulting from the use of this information.**

The trademarks that are used are without any consent, and the publication of the trademark is without permission or backing by the trademark owner. All trademarks and brands within this book are for clarifying purposes only, and are owned by the owners themselves, not affiliated with this document.

Introduction

Excellent, you want to create amazing pictures. This book is designed to help you create amazing pictures you will want to frame and hang on your wall or put on your desk. There are so many wonderful things to draw in this world, and it can sometimes be a chore to decide on images that will turn out amazing. You will see in this book that simplicity is key, simple moments and simple little details are some of the elements of amazing pictures.

All good art starts with simple inspiration. The next step is deciding what form or medium which you want to create in. It is important to have a quiet undisturbed place, or if being in the midst of busynessis what helps you be creative, find a loud crowded place and work away. It's up to you. Do whatever makes you feel comfortable and ready to create.

Art is where you are in control to be free. The amazing pictures in this book are created by building upon small little strokes, along with excellent outlines, to slowly form a beautiful finished product. You can use pencil first, which is important so that you can erase and perfect your line. Remember, it is all about practice. You will be better at creating lines the more lines you draw.

Drawing has a lot to do with the wrist. You want a fluidity with your wrist, so your wrists and hands enable you to slide across the page and lay down the pencil or ink so your image comes out looking clean. You can do this by building the small lines into large ones or connecting larger ones, whatever works for you, or whatever the drawing consists of.

Always remember to start your main subject matter in the proper place on the page. This way, when you step back from the page, the proportion makes sense, and the picture looks right. Remember that imperfect lines make up a drawing, because there are very few perfect lines in nature. The illusion of perfection is what we see in a beautiful picture. A great drawing is made with slightly crooked lines or slanted, and the appearance of the straight line is what we see. So let us take a look at some amazing drawings and create some art.

Chapter 1 – Preparing to Draw

Preparing to Draw

Drawing starts with you and your comfort. Pick a comfortable spot to draw, where there are very little distractions, unless you like distractions. You want a comfortable chair that makes you want to work, not sit back and sleep. You also want a nice hard surface that is clean and free from bumps.

You can use any pencil or pen to draw, but let me say that if you get a little better quality pencil or pen, it may be a bit easier to draw. Zebra makes really good pencils, and you can order them from the web. The best type of pen for making Steampunk is a paintbrush pen. The drawings in this book are created with a paintbrush pen. This is a pen that has a tip that bends like a paintbrush, and you can vary the darkness of the line as well as the girth. You can find these pens at your local craft or art stores. You can actually buy a set of paint brush pens from Crayola online. You may also use a pen, but in the beginning, you may want to use a pencil so that you can correct your mistakes.

Paper is the same. You want to practice on cheap paper, but you don't have to. You can buy an inexpensive drawing book if you want to see your progression. Paper does not cost that much money, so if it inspires you to buy a nicer paper to draw on, go for it. You want to draw on paper that has no lines. If you feel that you want to frame your drawings when they are done, then use a piece of loose paper that will fit into a frame that can easily hang on your wall.

If you go to an art store or the craft store, instead of using a pink eraser on the end of a pencil, they make a fabulous white eraser that makes the least amount of marks on your paper. You want to get a couple of those. It's easier to have the eraser off of the pencil, and the white erasers have a larger surface, so it is easier and doesn't wear down as fast. These little things make a difference, so you can concentrate and make the best picture you can.

Pick a time when you are alert and feel good when you want to draw. You don't want to be tired, because art can be a little frustrating at first. You are training yourself to do something. You won't be perfect at first, so be in a willing mood, and you are up for the best chance at success. Now that you have your tools, let us take a look at how to draw six fabulous Steampunk drawings.

Chapter 2 Woman with Wrap

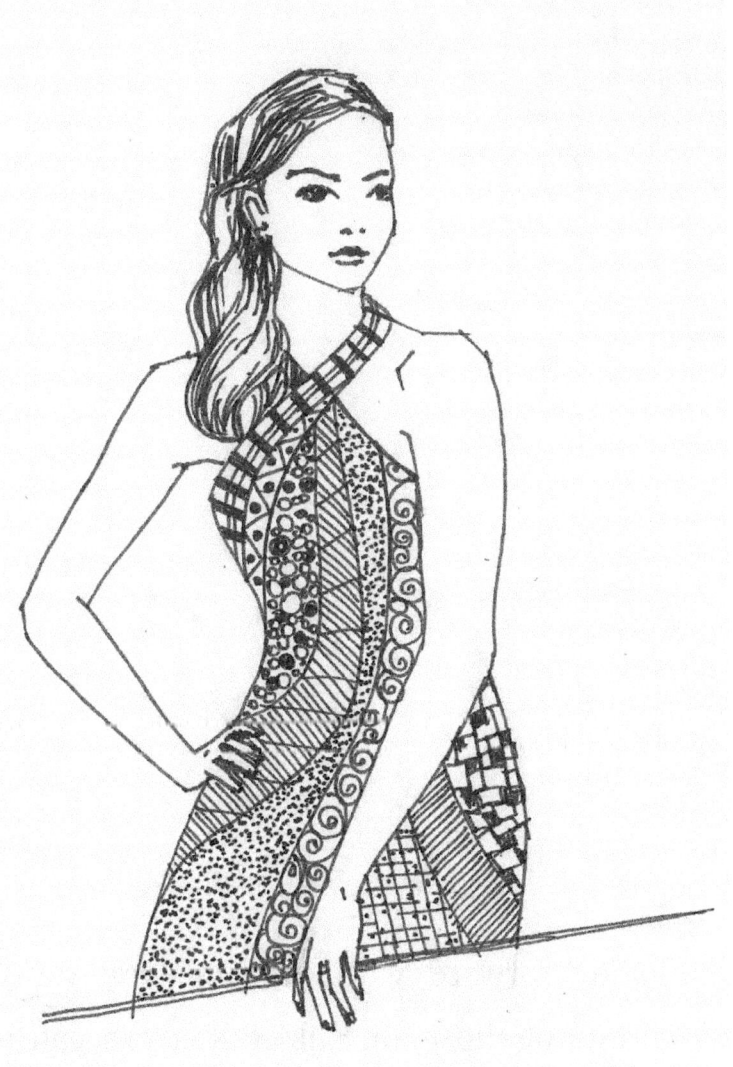

Step One

Before moving forward with drawing, you want a general outline of the main subject, as you can see here you are a making lines starting from the top sketching out her head. You then build the structure of her body with the lines going out wide to the side so you get the proportion right on the entire paper. Notice the outline of her face and the slight slants of each line. This is all important. Erase if you have to, until you get the gist of the slightness of each line.

Step Two

You see here that some of the lines have been
replaced and new ones drawn, because some lines are
just for guides. In all these drawings, you want to
study the first completed drawing and after you start

your drawing, look at your paper after each step. Check your drawing with the one in the book, and make sure that your lines match. You want to watch for proportion. Also, take a step back often, so that you are seeing exactly what is on your paper. You can see the outline of the hair in this drawing. Build your lines up from a single line, and then add more for depth and range.

Step Three

Step three is filling in more detail. You want to watch all angles of your lines. Part of what makes this drawing dynamic and amazing is the variation of the lines. The lines slope in different directions, and style. Curves of the shoulder, curl in the hair, and the cross of the shirt. Notice that you are not creating perfect straight lines. These lines are built up, and have subtle arches and curves. You want to pay close attention to this.

Step Four

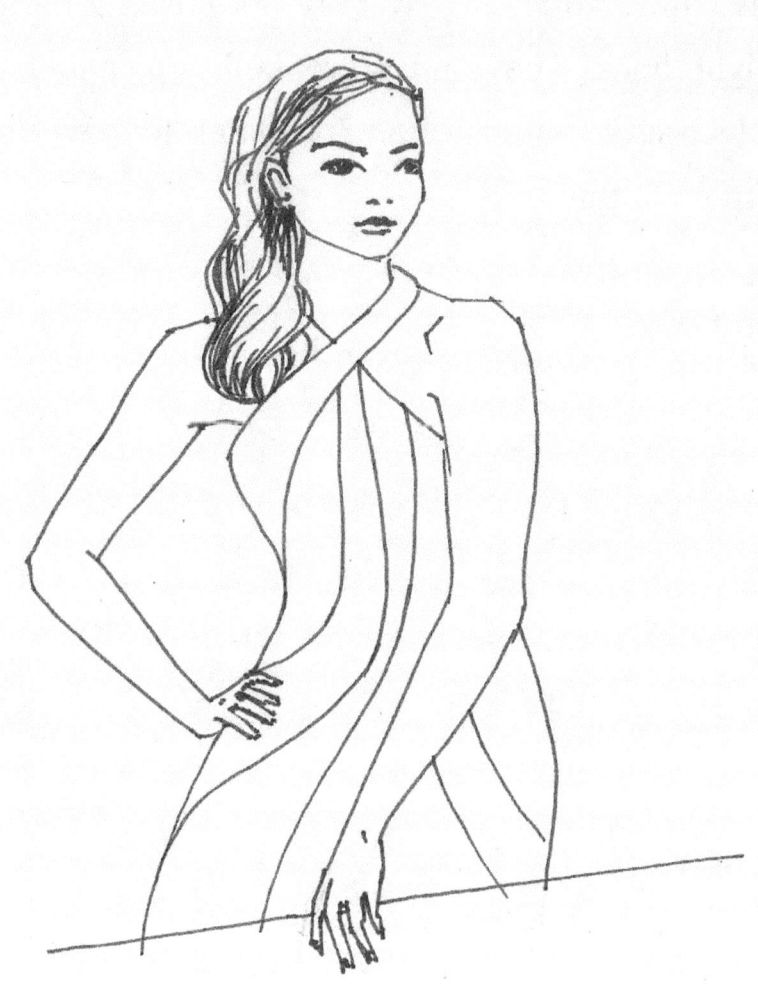

In step four, you are going to clear away the unwanted lines until you have a clean picture, and then you will go over the drawing in ink. You can see the difference of this drawing and all the lines in the previous drawing. The lines are for the structure, because the most important thing is the proportion of your drawing. The size of the head and the thickness of the arm. Do not worry if you have to erase to get it all looking the way it should.

Step Five

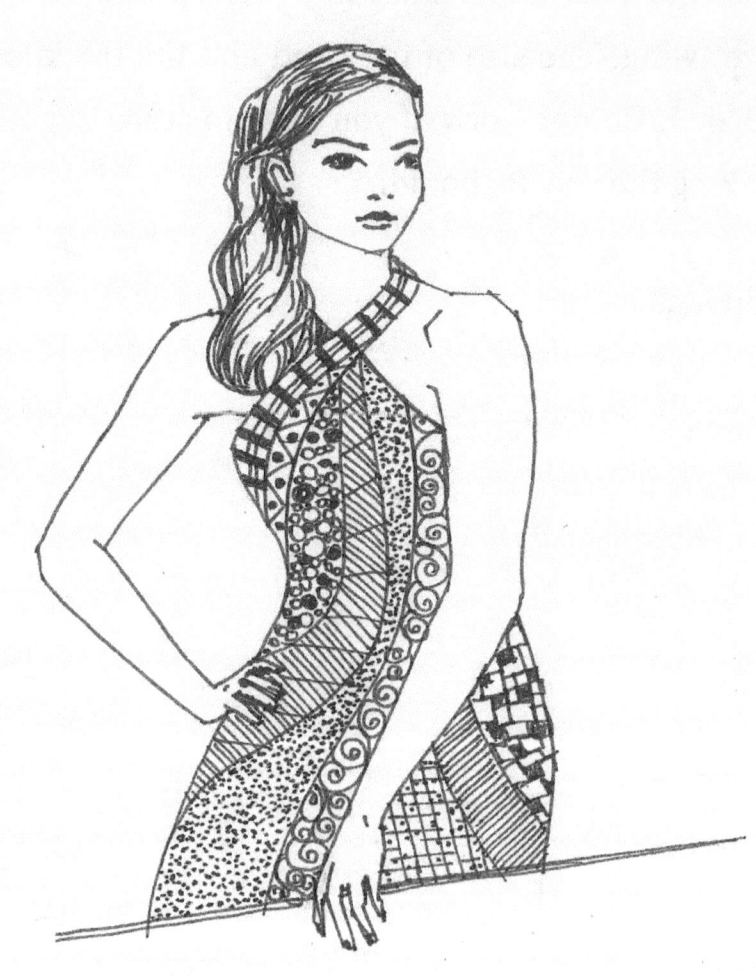

In this final step, you will add the detail of the dress. You want to pay close attention to the direction of the lines. They have a subtle slant, and turn in different directions. You are going to create the lines first, and then fill in with the details. Notice the different patterns of dots, swirls, stripes, zigzag, circles, and more. Match the pattern and repeat.

Chapter Three - Seated Lady

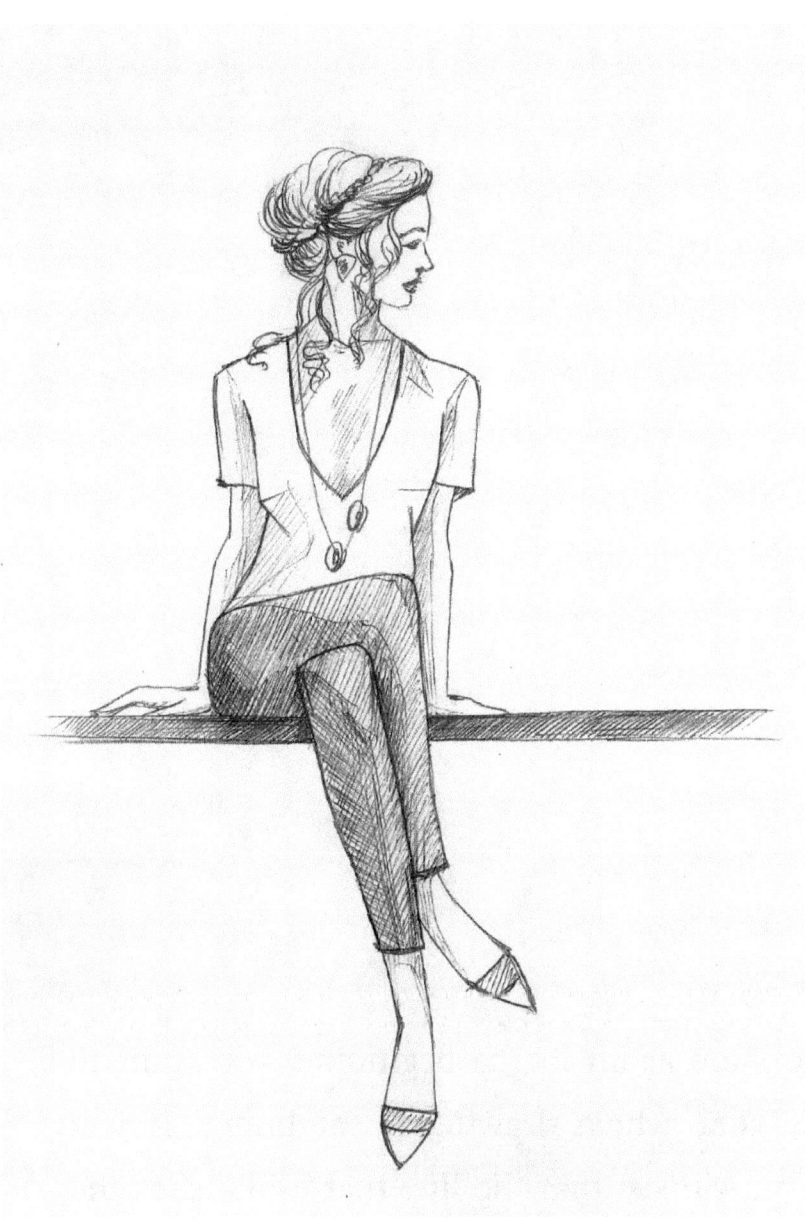

Step One

Step one, here again in the beginning, you want to structure your whole drawing by outlining. If you notice, you will see that the line that establishes the angle of her body is drawn slightly to the right of the center, and the line is angled slightly on an up slope from left to the right. More than three quarters of the way down is your horizontal line, which will be the impression of the seat she is sitting on. Watch the distances between the lines of the legs, so the legs have enough depth to look like legs.

Step Two

In step three, you will be adding the shoulders and the head. Watch your angles and subtle slants of the lines. They make all the difference in the world for the gentleness of the picture. It's fine to build each line slowly if you have to, just connect each part so it looks like a line, but you are eventually putting ink over the pencil so the pencil lines don't have to be perfect. You are also adding the head. You can see it is a side angle. Just build the chin with small lines, paying attention to the difference between the straight lines and the curves.

Step Three

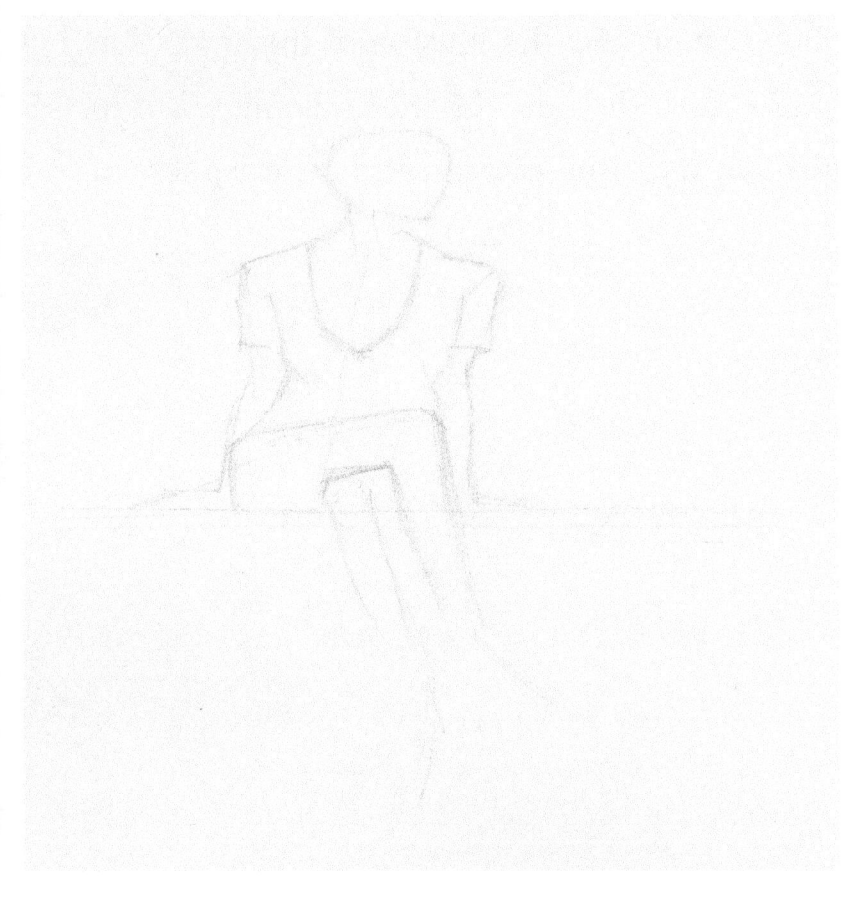

Step three is very important, because you are getting thigh in and her clothes. Notice the shape of the thigh. It is an odd shape, but it looks like a thigh. Make sure that the lines are curved on the side. The curve makes it look like a soft thigh. You may have to erase and redraw a few times to get the thickness right, but just copy the odd shape, and build with the small lines. Also add her shirt, and the lines going beyond her arm creates the illusion of the shirt. You them squarer than the line of her arm going down to distinguish between the soft skin and the crispness of cotton.

Step Four

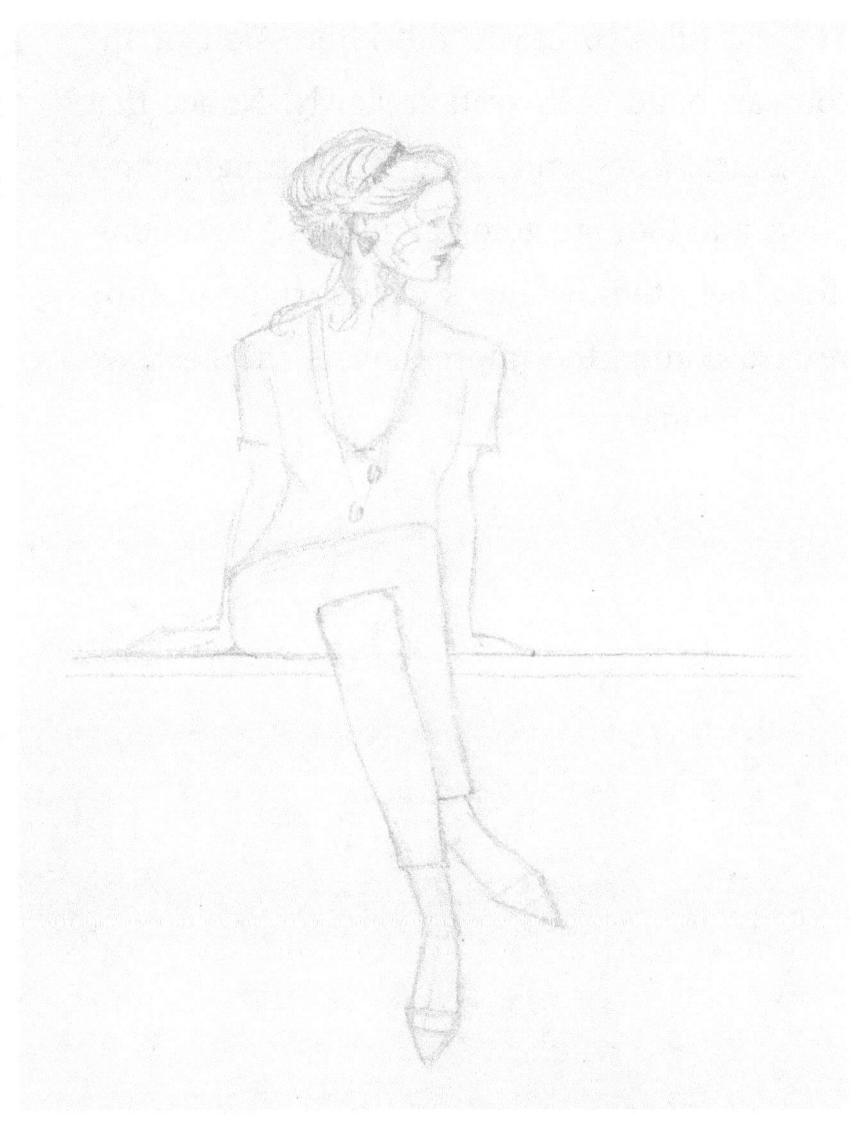

Step four is about adding her hair. You are creating the puff of her hair with the curved lines and the head band impression. As with all, focus on the main parts of the body you want to see and draw all the different angles of the lines to create the impression of the hair. You can build each section slowly. Notice that you have slanted lines, and a somewhat straight and a curved line, and they are going in different directions. These lines help the dynamics of the whole picture. You are also adding the impression of the necklace with the two pendants.

Step Five

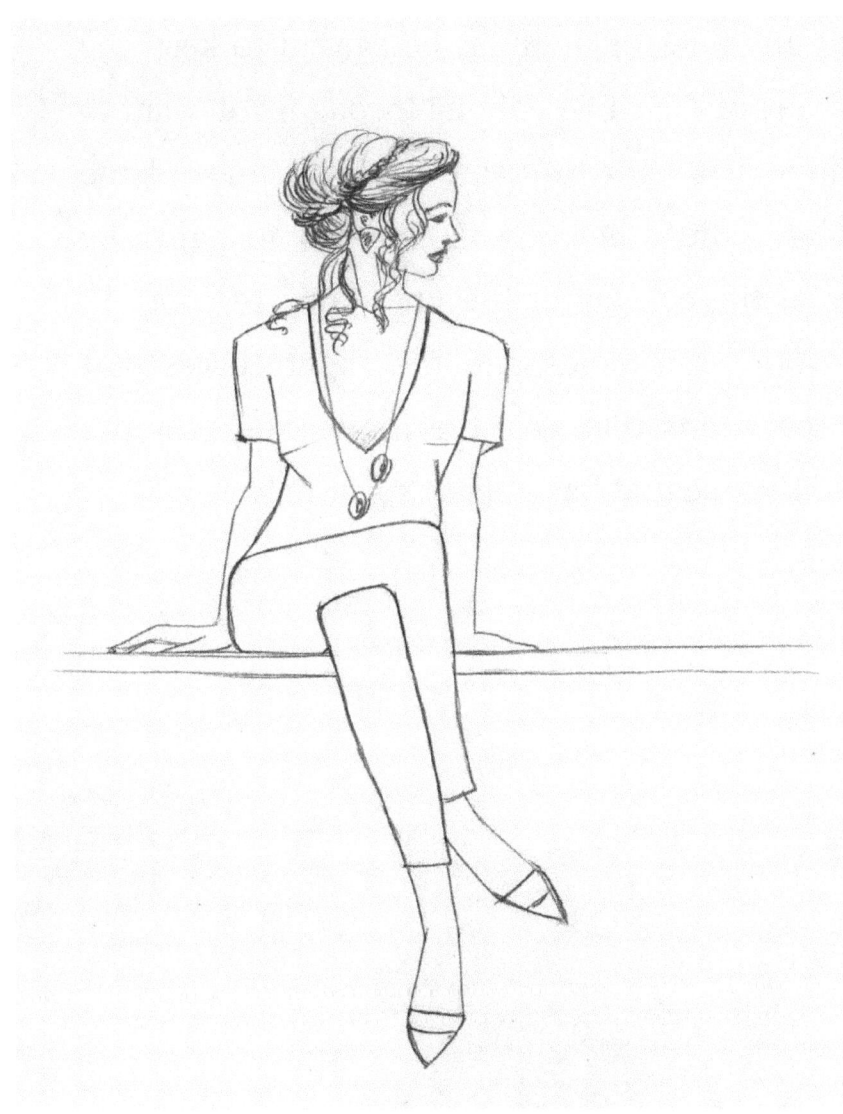

Step five, it's time for ink, and you will erase all other guidelines. If you are using the white eraser mentioned in Chapter one, it should not be too difficult to clean up the drawing. When you are drawing the lines of the hair, be careful to keep the slight white of the paper coming through. You want to get your wrists light to create the light lines of the hair. Plan a little before you put pen to paper by looking at the curving of the lines you are about to draw. Notice the hands and the slight curves that create the hands that give the impression they are flat, and the one that has a slight space between.

Step Six

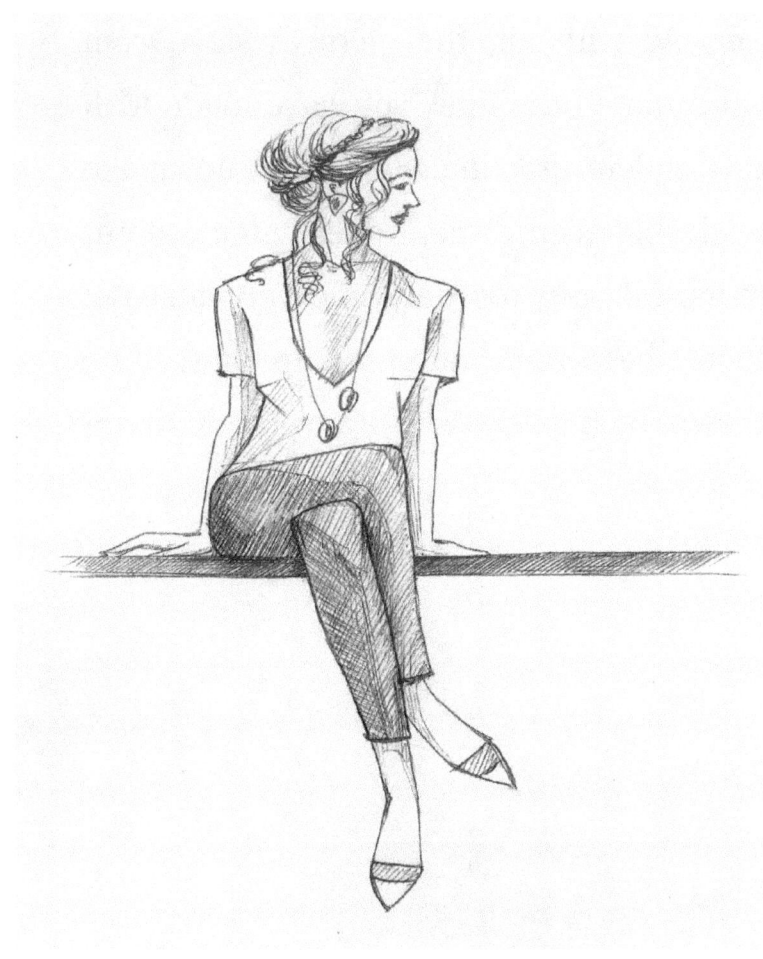

Step Six is all about adding the shade and depth to the picture by hatching lines. You are simply drawing straight lines next to each other on a slant to create the illusion of shadows and darker shades. Then to get even darker shades, you will change the angle of the lines and lay the different angled lines on top of the first layer. As with all, the pictures start from head to toe and match the lines you have made with those of the complete drawing. Be careful not make your line too dark, because there does come a point where too much ink gets too dark and you can't see the contrast. Just keep your hand pressure on the line light, and you will be fine.

Chapter Four - Girl and the Moon

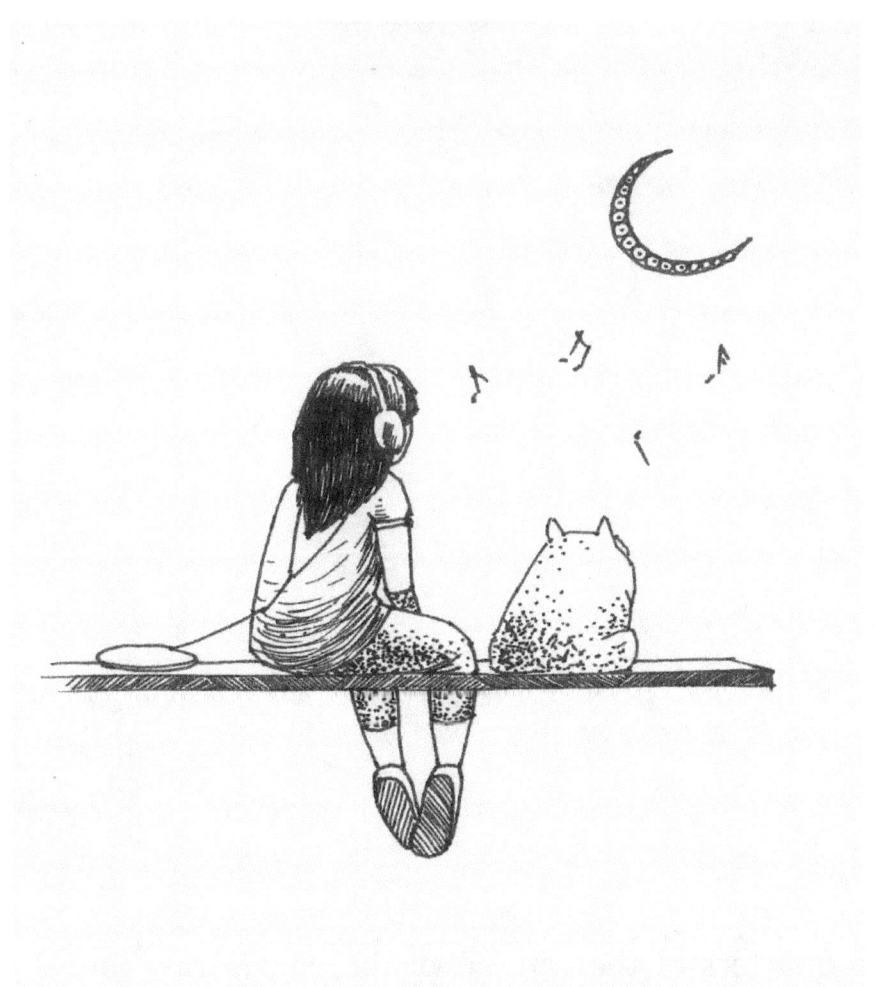

Step One

Three quarters of the way down the page, draw the lines for the bench and the outline of the girl and the cat.

Step Two

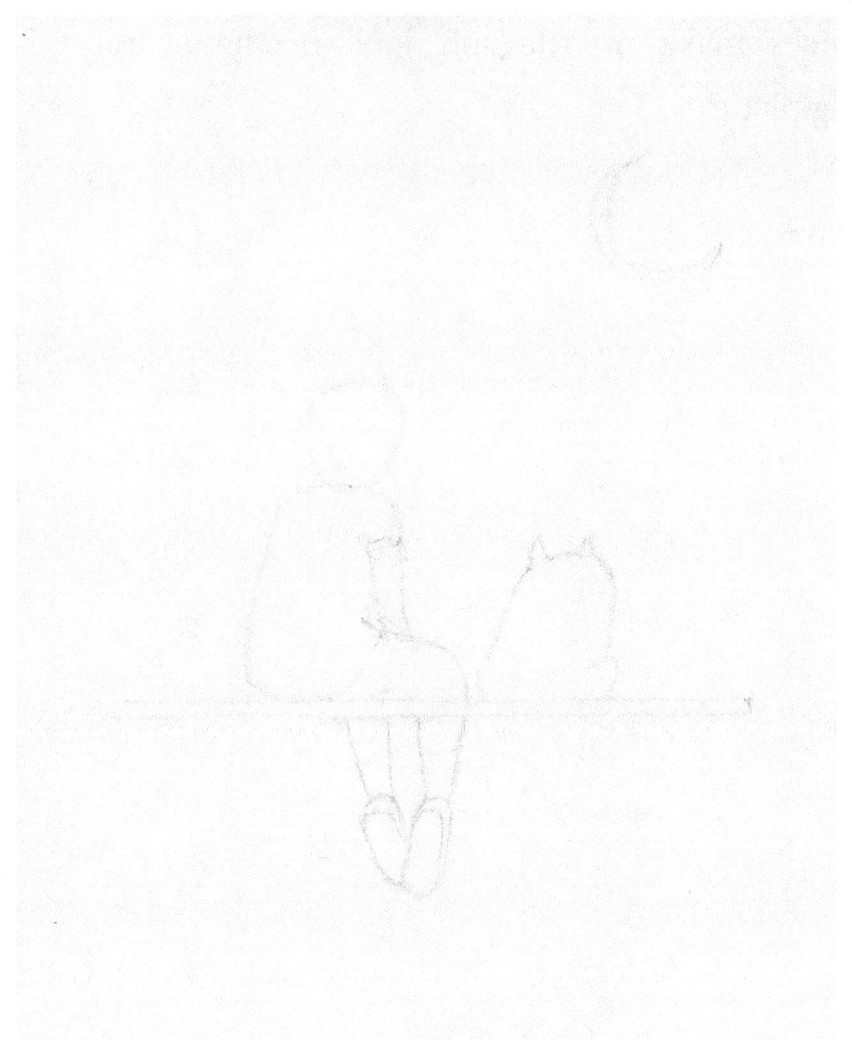

Step two, you are adding a little detail of her dangling legs and the moon. The cat also gets ears and such. Pay close attention to the slight curves and subtle angles of each line. In this picture, these little differences make up the soft look of the overall amazing picture.

Step Three

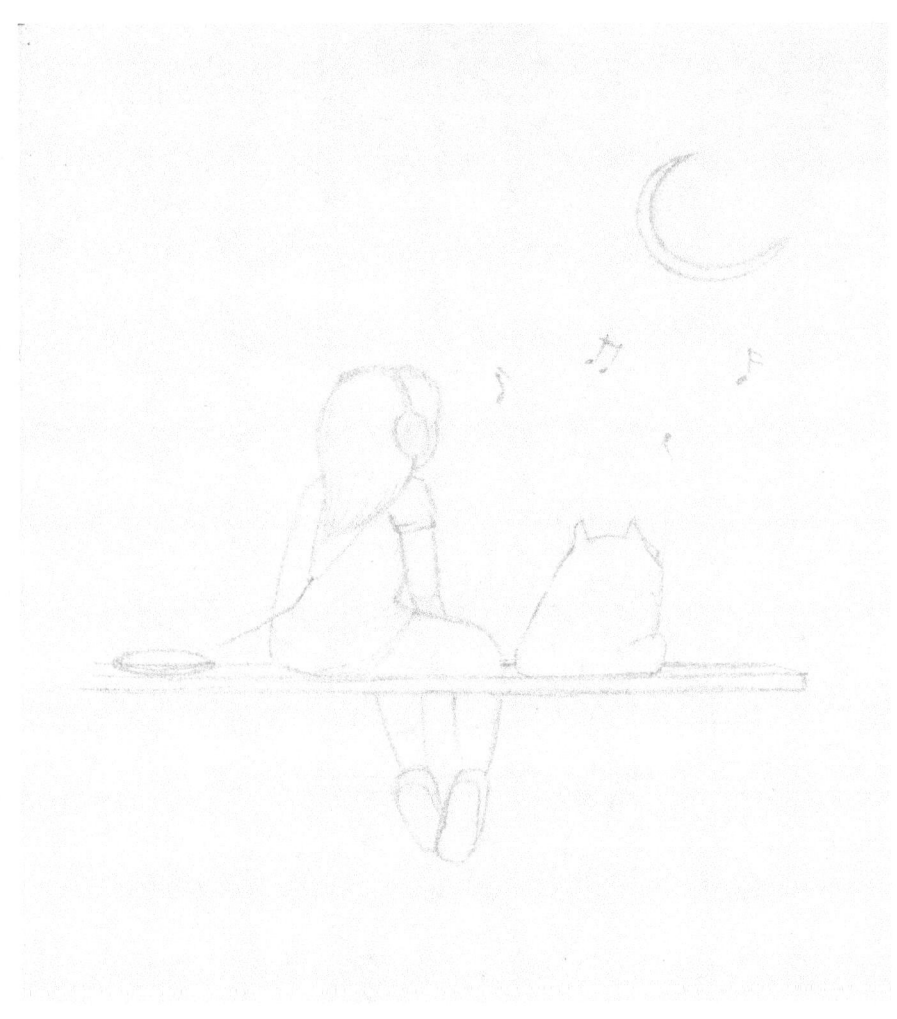

Step three, you are drawing in her music player, her hair detail, headphones, and music notes. Be conscious of the curved lines, and the extra detail lines for shading.

Step Four

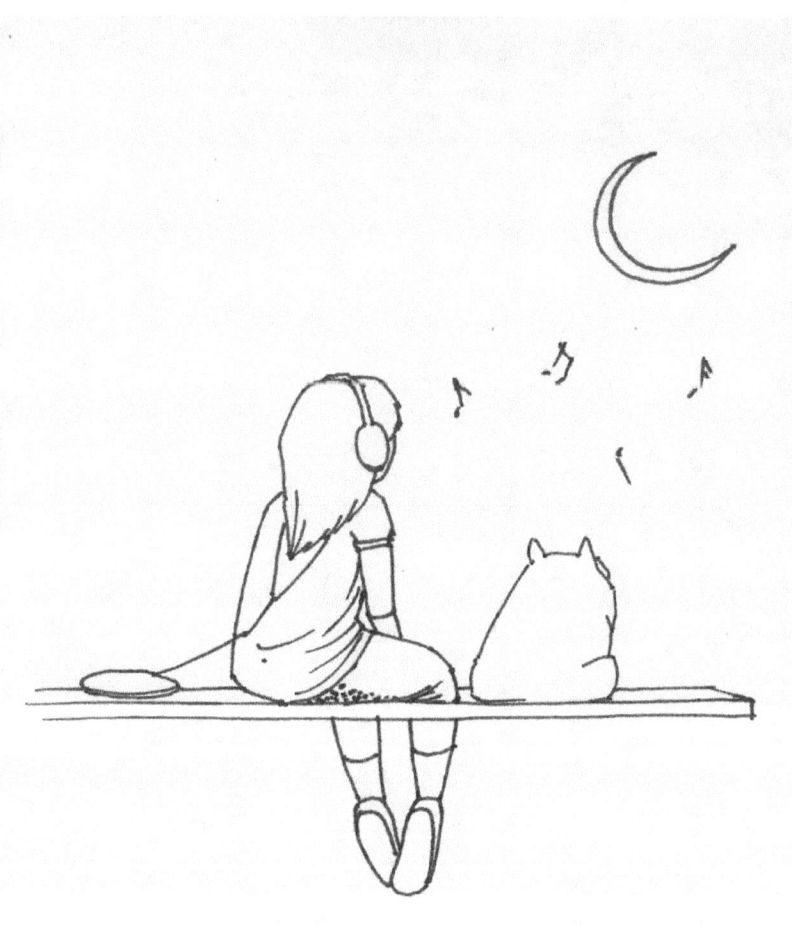

Step four, it is time for the ink. You will get rid of any excess lines, and then go over your pencil lines with pen. You can build each long line with small ones.

Step Five

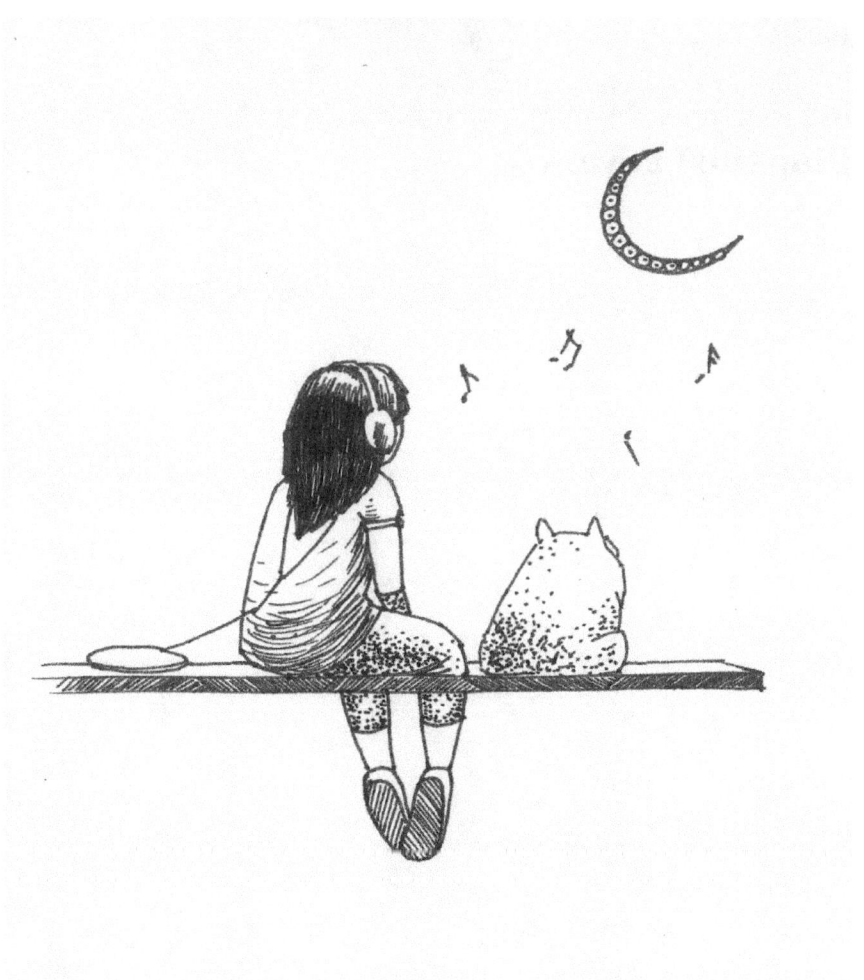

Step five is all about filling in the shading and detail. Lay each line down neatly and quickly. Watch out for going too dark. Her pants details are just dots. Get the curve in the shade of her shirt. The bench side is darkened with the different direction hatching lines. The moon is simply detailed with small circles and a dot inside.

Smelling the Flowers

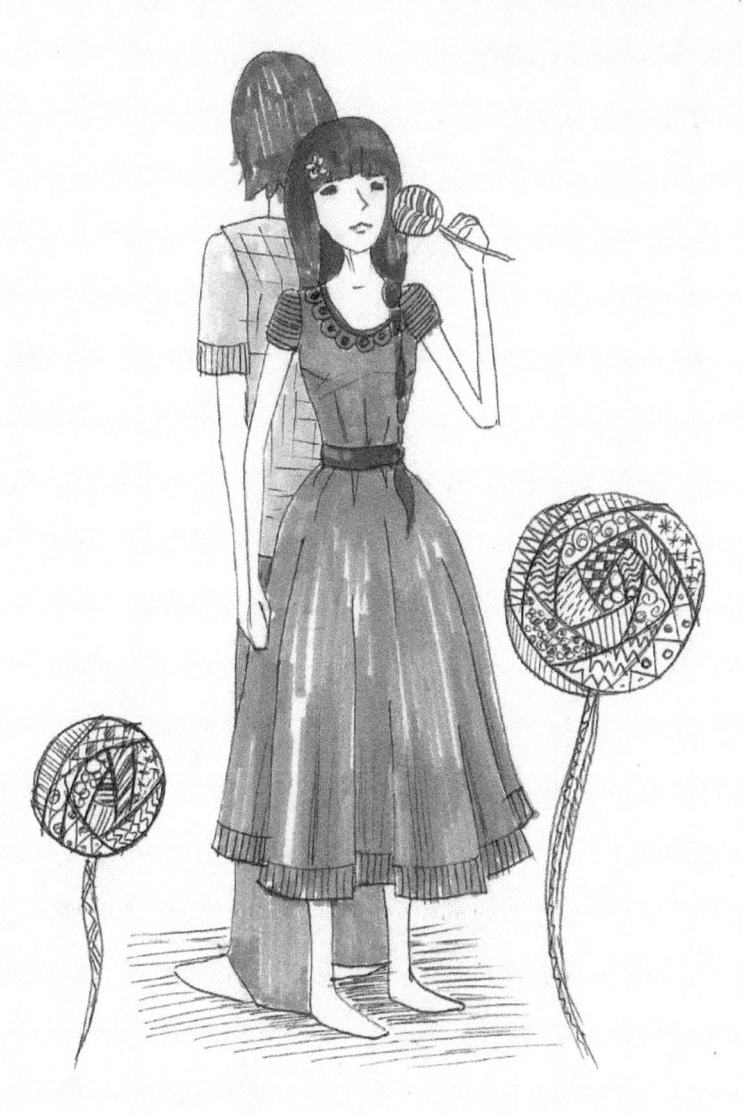

Step One

This picture is slightly different as it has color, and the beginning is the same with simple structure lines not quite in the center, but you are establishing the angle of the girl.

Step Two

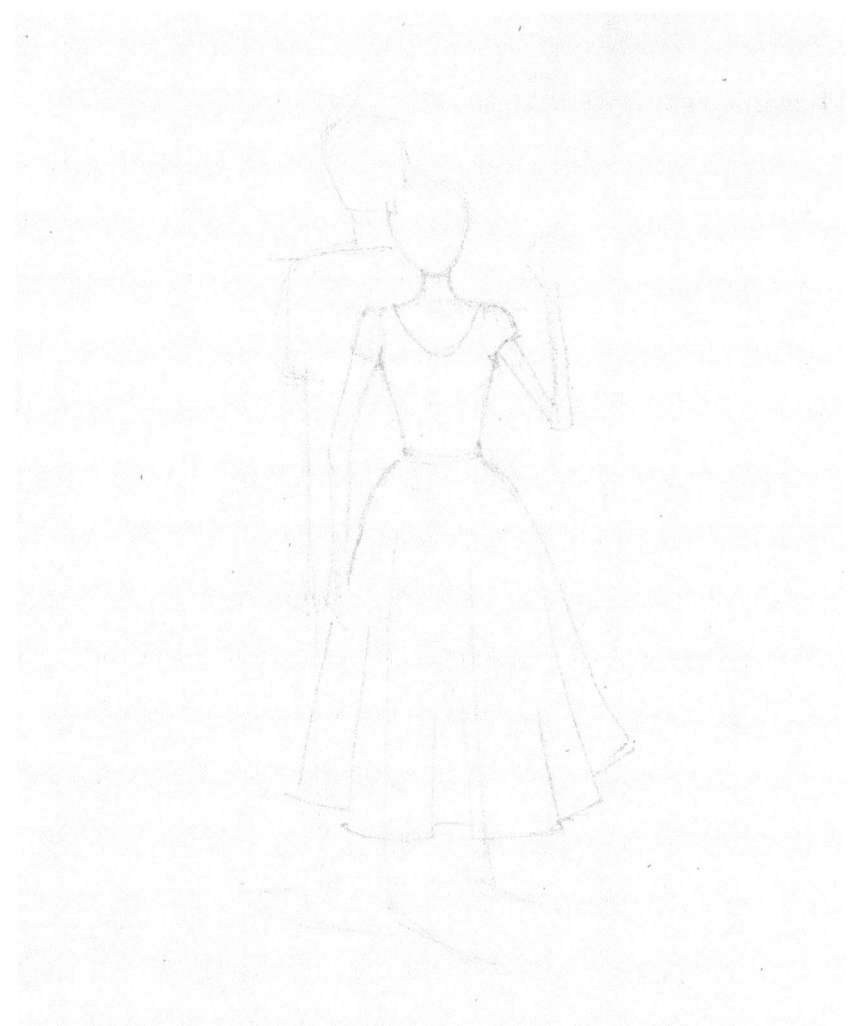

Step Two, you are adding the body and skirt. The lines are curved in the skirt, and straighter for the body. Build them slowly and consistently. You are also adding the man behind her. Use her as a guide to draw his lines so they are attached and look right.

Step Three

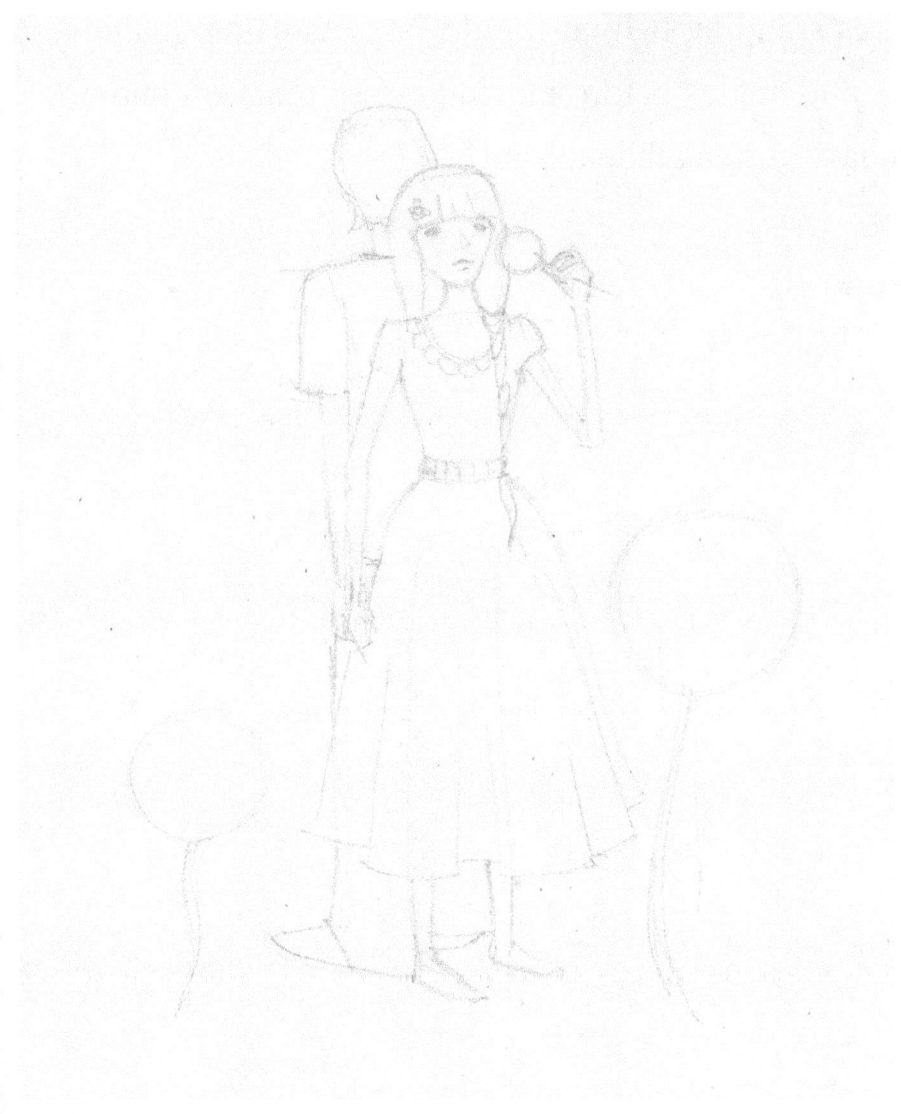

Step Three is the addition of a few more details. You will add in the flower she is smelling, as well as the flowers in front of her. Make note that the flowers are drawn large, allowing for the appearance of the two figures standing behind the flowers. As usual, match lines and angles before moving on, so that you know you have gotten all details in.

Step Four

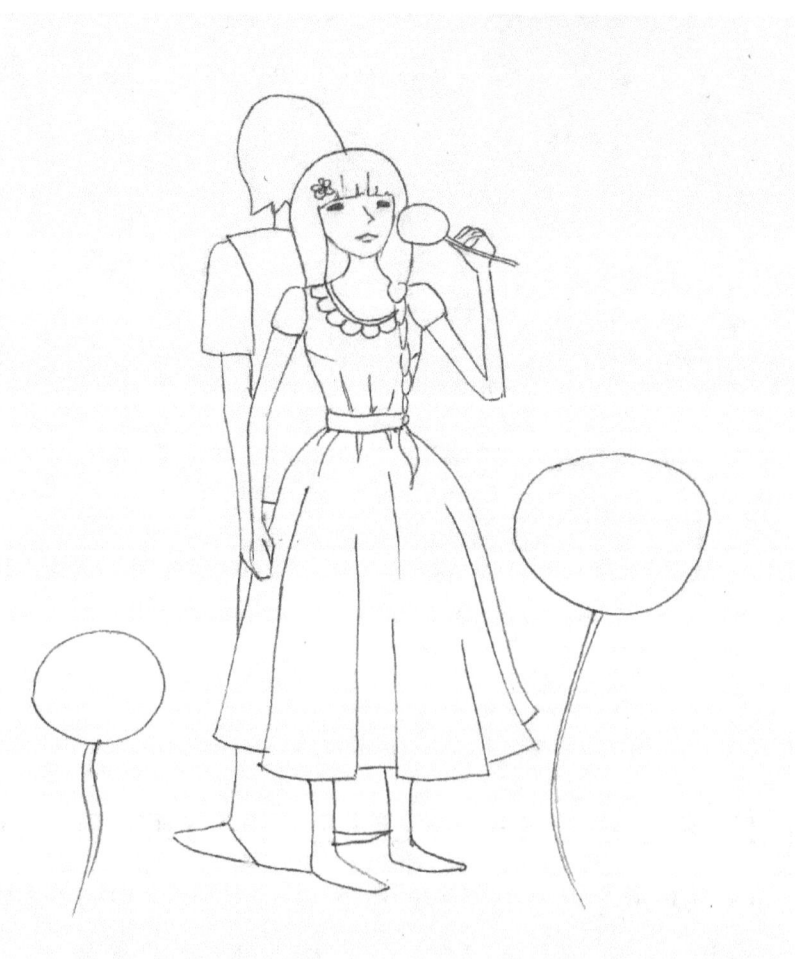

Step four, it is time for ink. Follow the most sensible lines, and erase the remaining ones. Facial features are very small and subtle. Take a look at the angles and distance between each facial feature.

Step Five

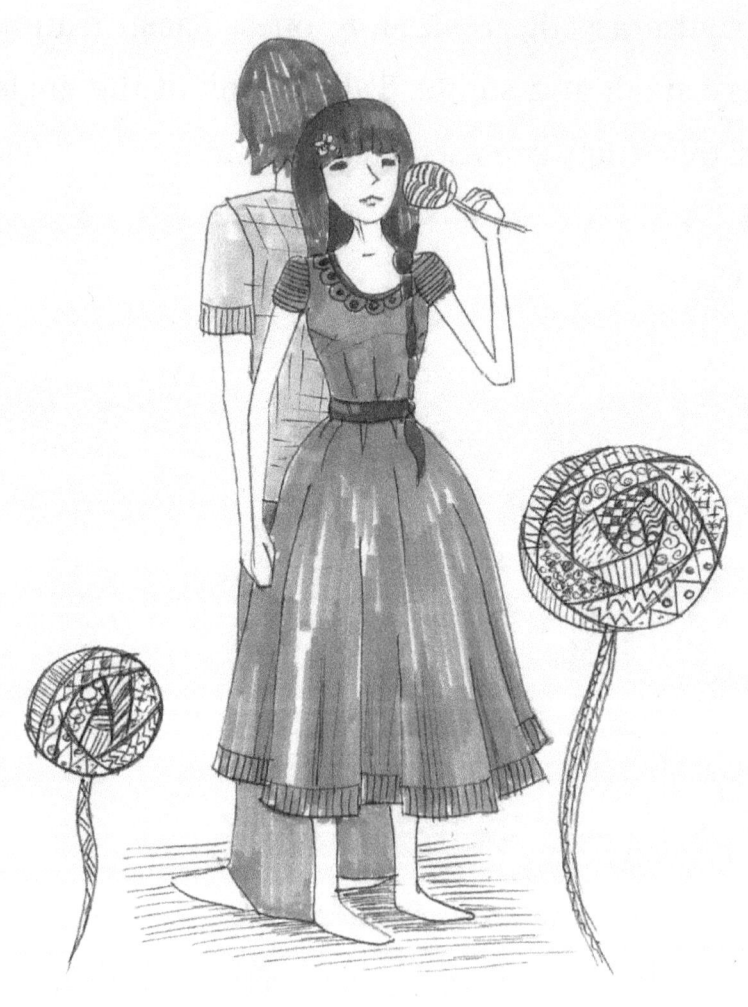

This final step is all about the color and design to the flowers. Any black detail will be drawn over the color. Make sure when you do this that you allow the colored marker to dry before you add the black ink so no running occurs. In the flowers, draw your angled lines first, and then fill in the designs.

Chapter Six - Carrying Cake

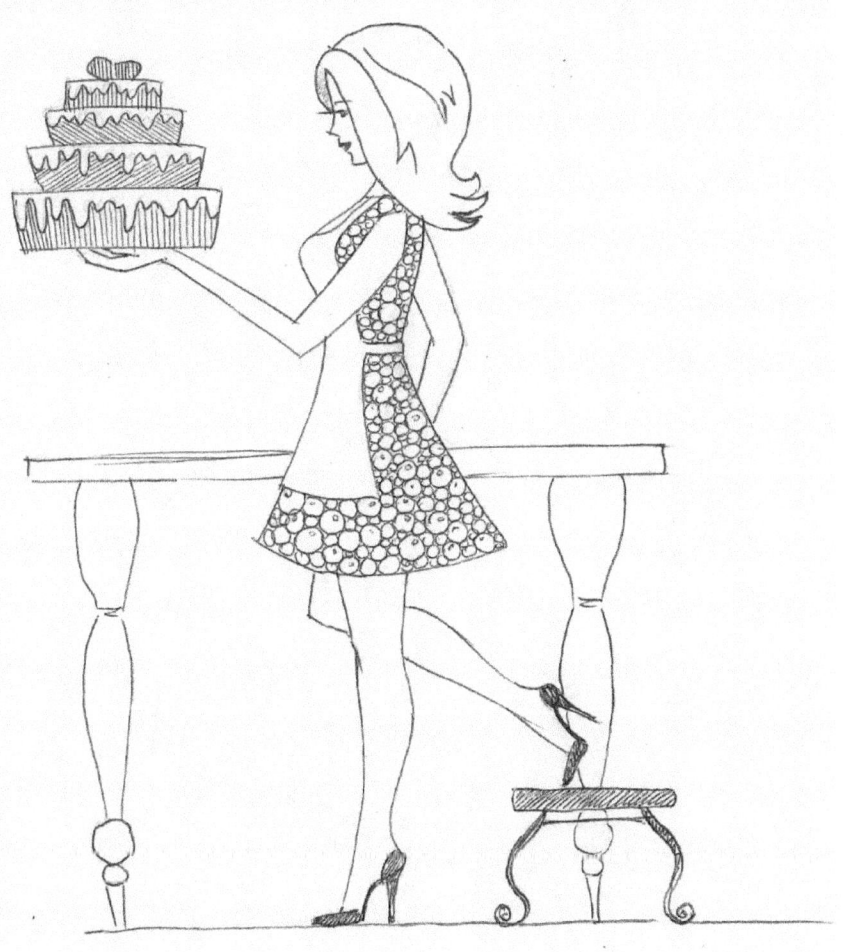

Step One

Step one, build the essential direction of the figure not quite in the center as usual. Leave room for the cake and table on the paper.

Step Two

Step Two, you are building the bulk of her body, as well as some of her dress. Watch the angles of the lines and the distance so you are creating a substantial mass on the paper.

Step Three

Here you are adding the curve of her hair and the rest of her dress. You will also build her high heels with small lines.

Step Four

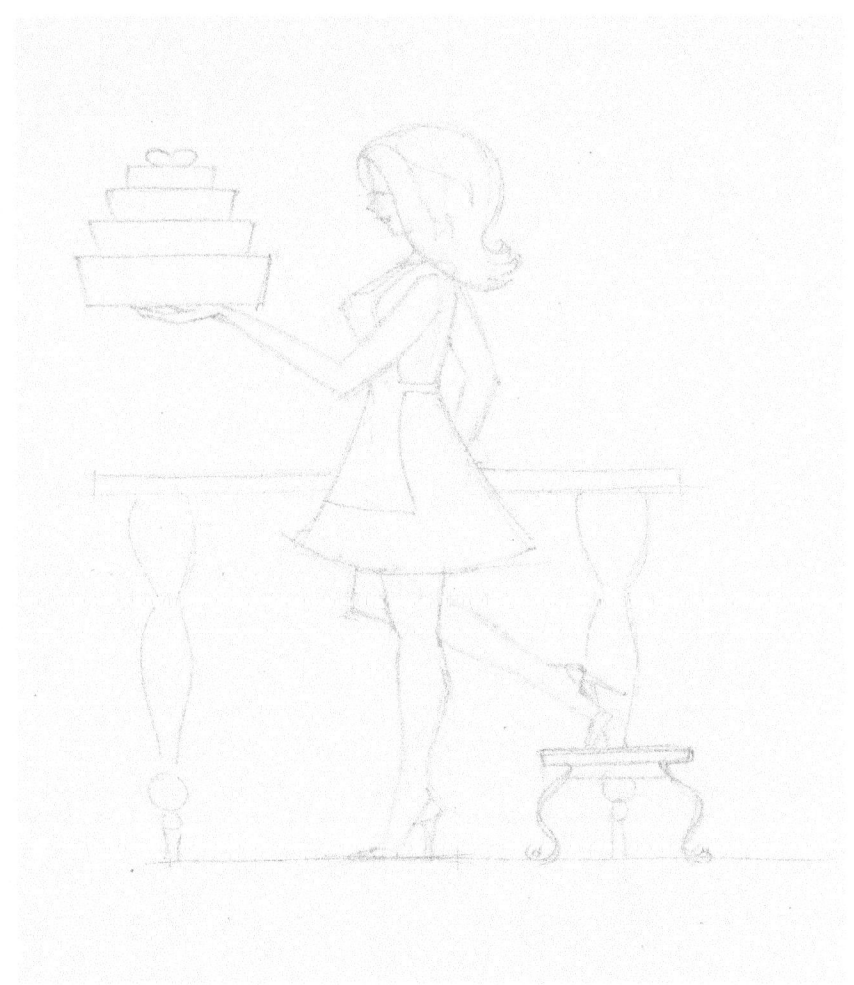

Step four, it is time for the variegated cake. You are making each cake layer with a smaller line until you get to the top. In this step, you will add the table. See how free and fluid the lines are for the table legs with the slight design.

Step Five

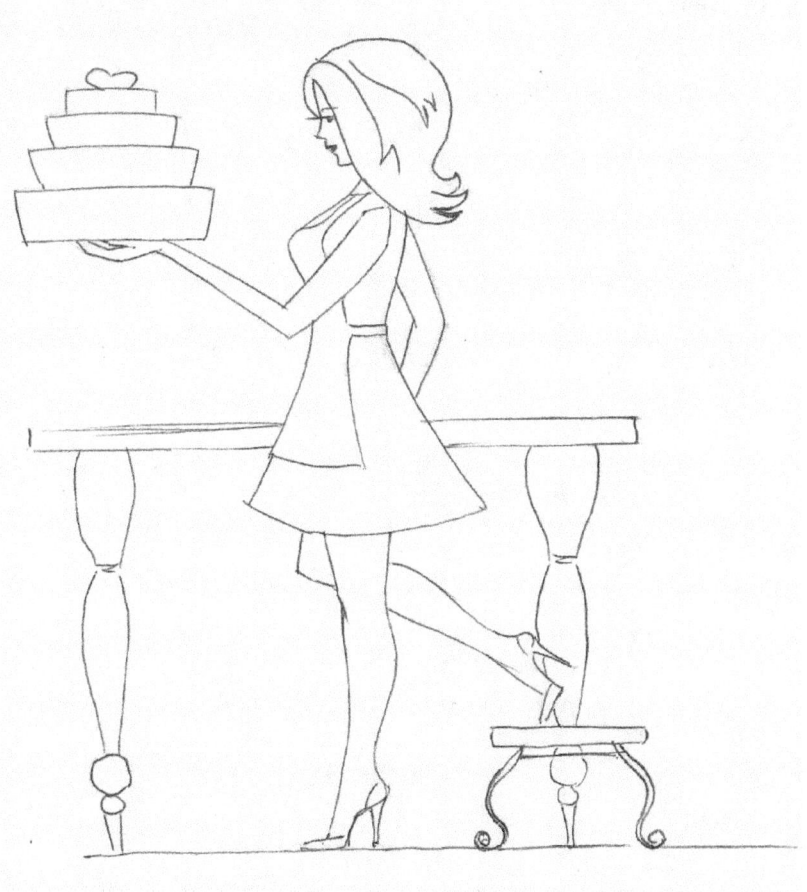

In step five, it is time for ink. Before you do, compare
your picture with this one, and make sure your pencil
drawing is close to this. You want to make sure the
lines are straight and square where they need to be,

and curved where they are supposed to be. Check angles as well.

Step Six

Carrying Cake

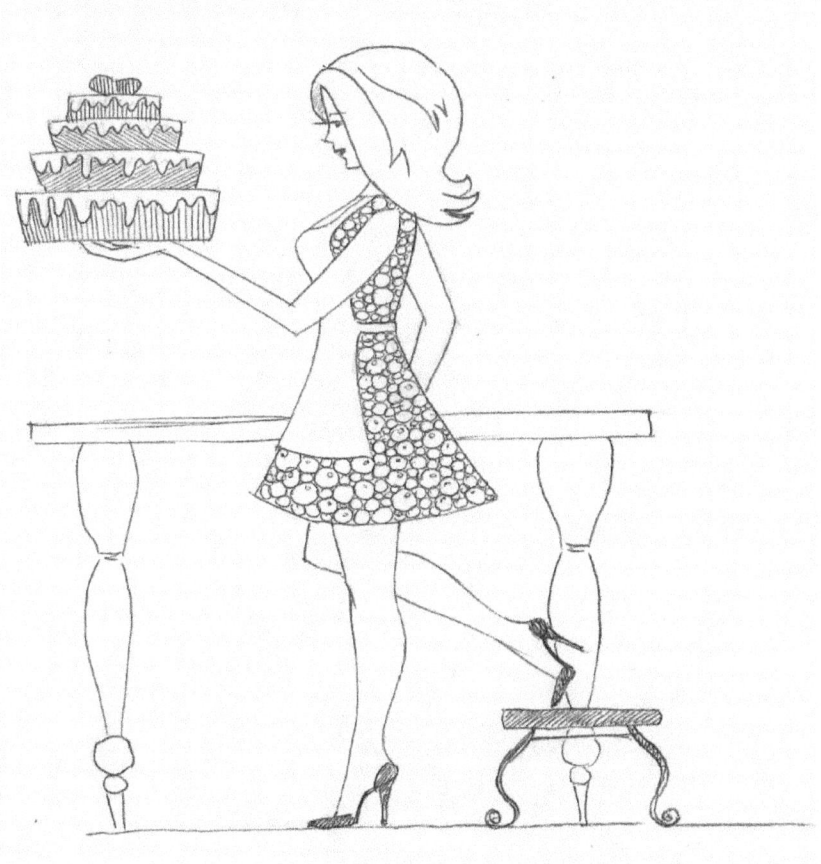

This final step is the fun part where you are filling in the details of this amazing picture. Here dress design is basically different size circles with a dot in between. You want to lay each graphic fluidly and clean. Hatching is used again in the shade of the table.

Chapter Seven - Artist with Animals

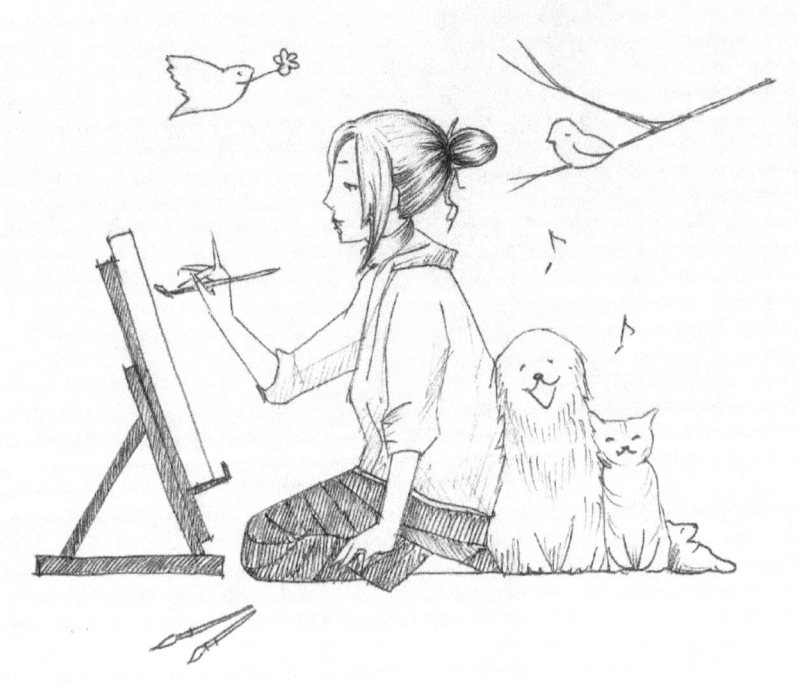

Step One

Step one is another chance to practice on the proper proportion of your drawing. You are drawing a line towards the bottom of the paper, and take note of the angles of the lines of the body of both the figure and the animals. Draw all lines according to what you see.

Step Two

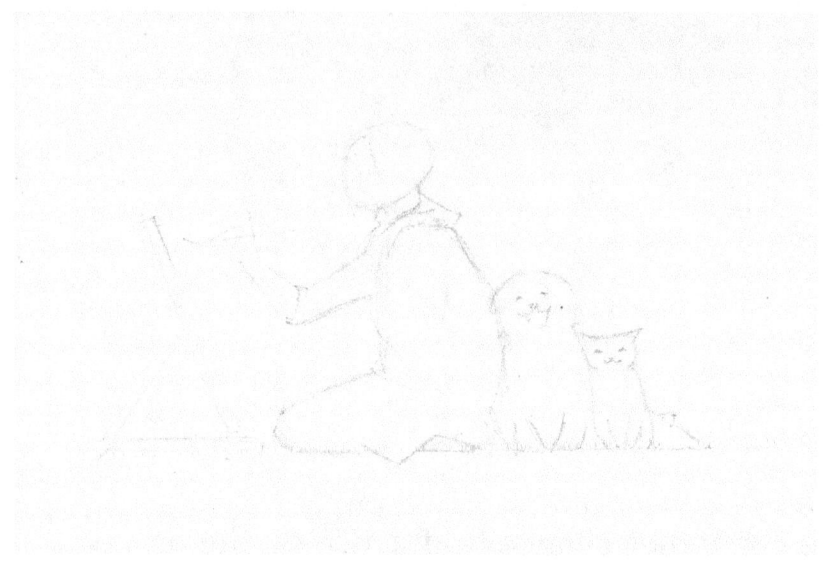

In this step, add the extra details like the face of the animals and a little more detail of the artist. See the curve of her back, and the angle of the lines in the arm, and make sure that your lines are close to the same.

Step Three

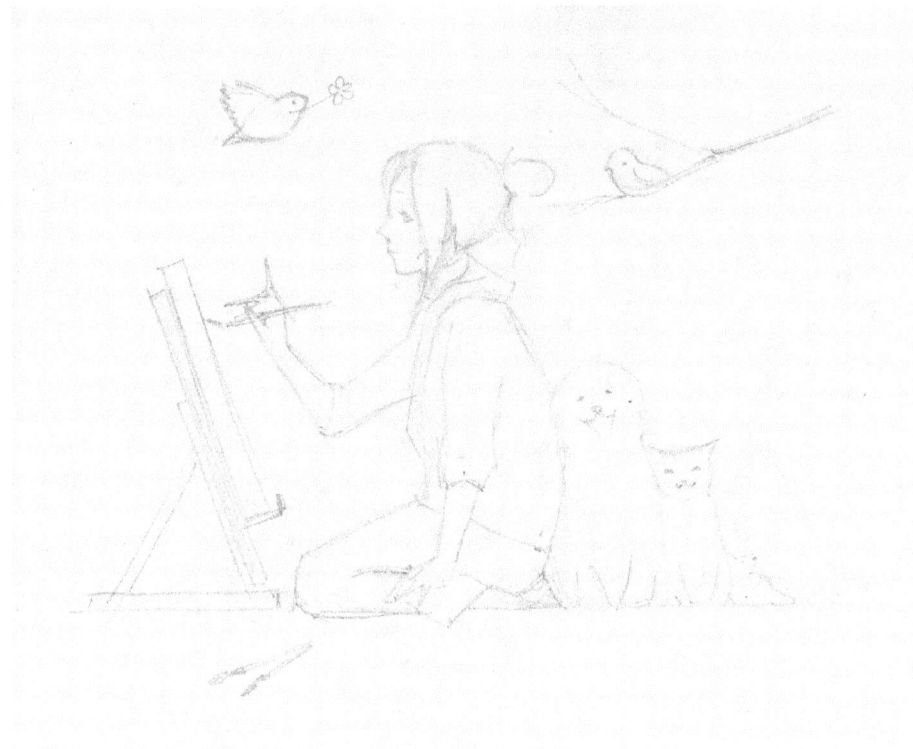

Now it is time for more detail on the girl. Make the face feature subtle and light. You are adding a little depth to the easel, and the addition of birds is a nice touch. This is a good time to check your picture with this one to see that you have all the lines correct.

Step Four

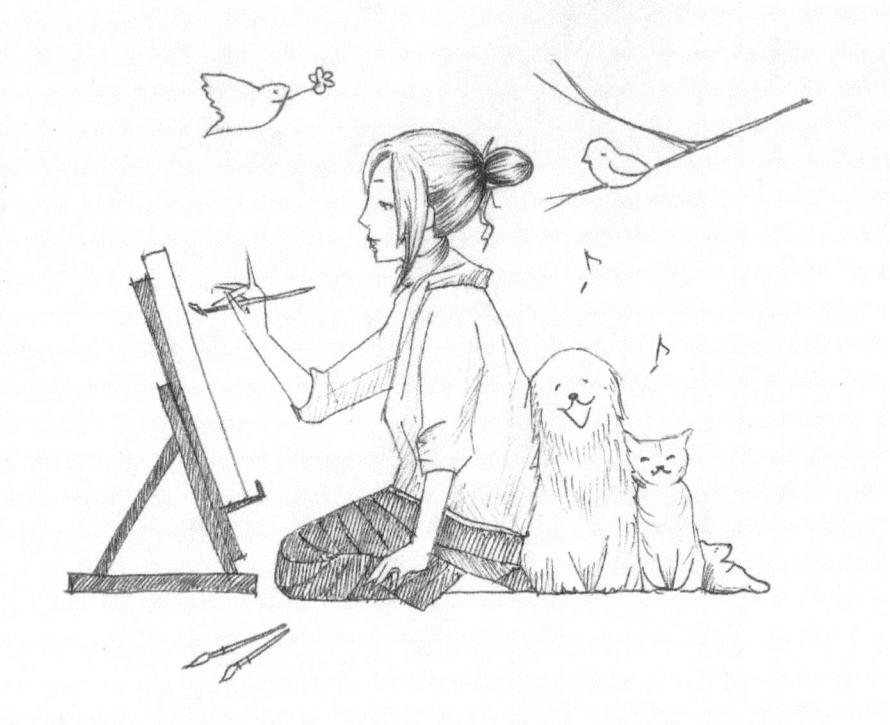

It is time for the final ink. You will take away the excess lines and add the pen ink for contrast and shine. You are using a single angled hatching line to create the shades in the picture, and don't forget the light angle lines in the dog's fur.

Chapter Eight – Star

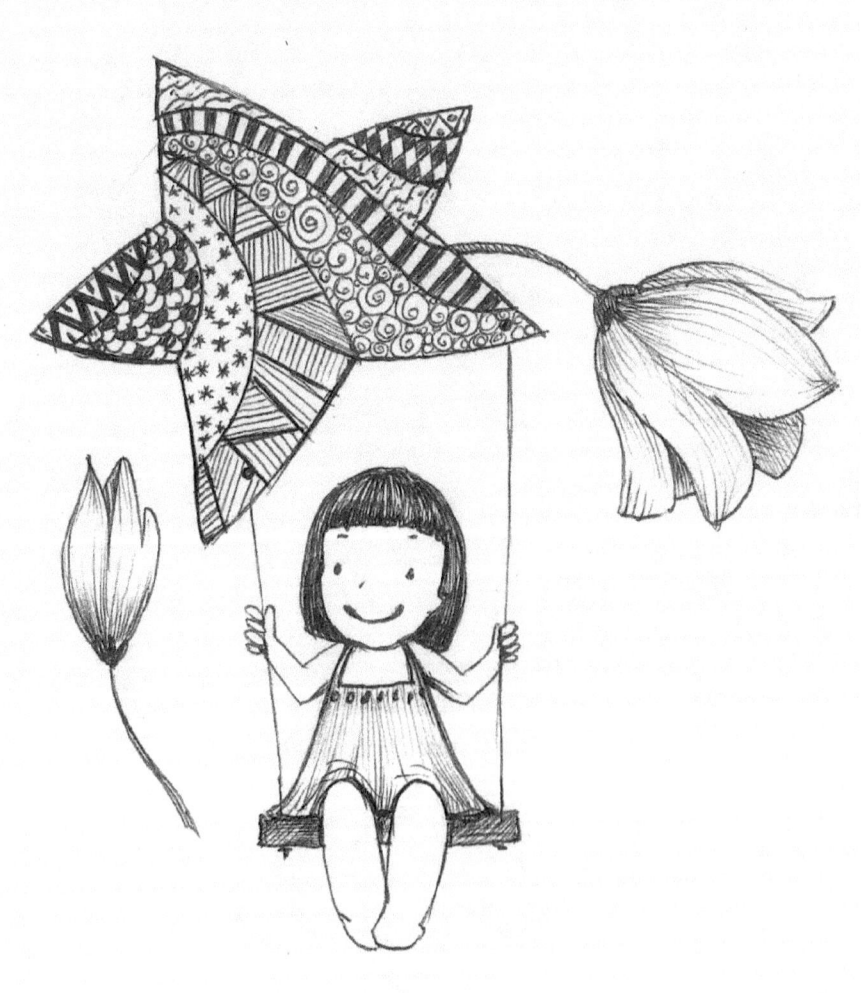

Step One

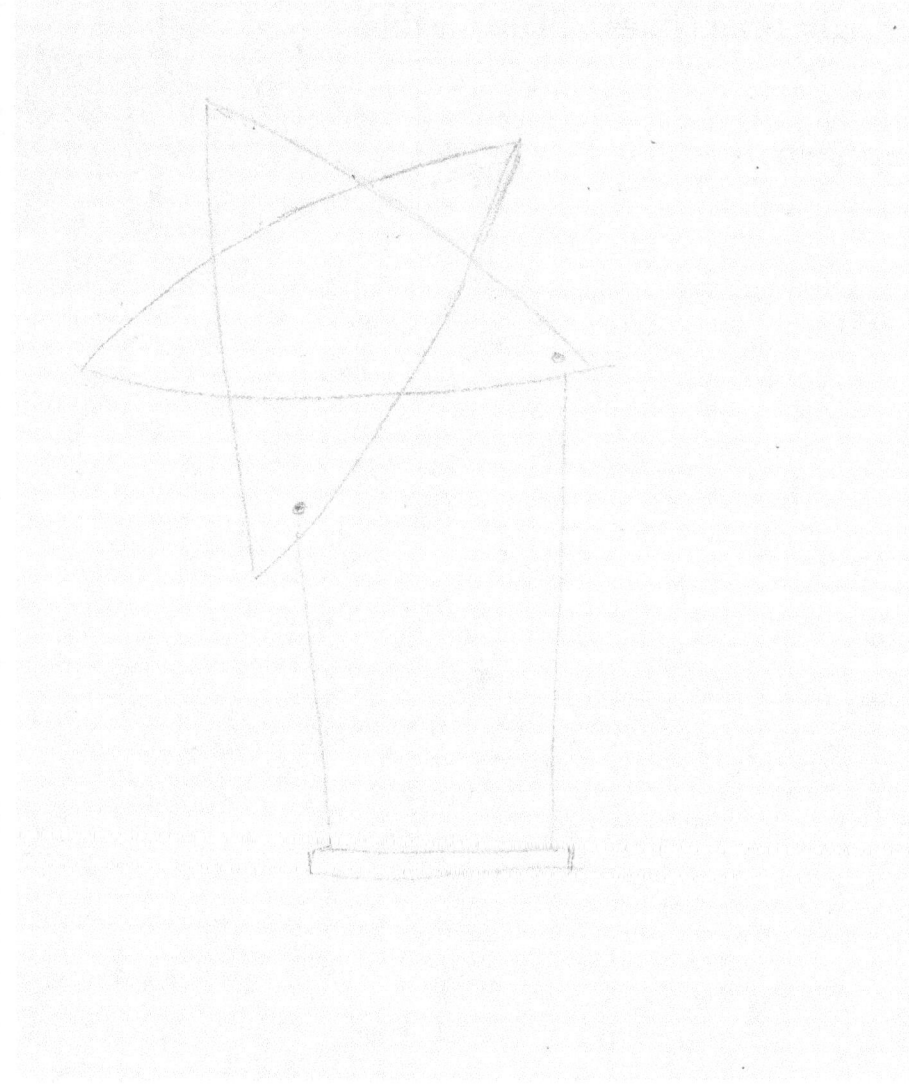

You are simply positioning the star and the swing both leaning more towards the left side of the page. Just light pencil lines will do for this.

Step Two

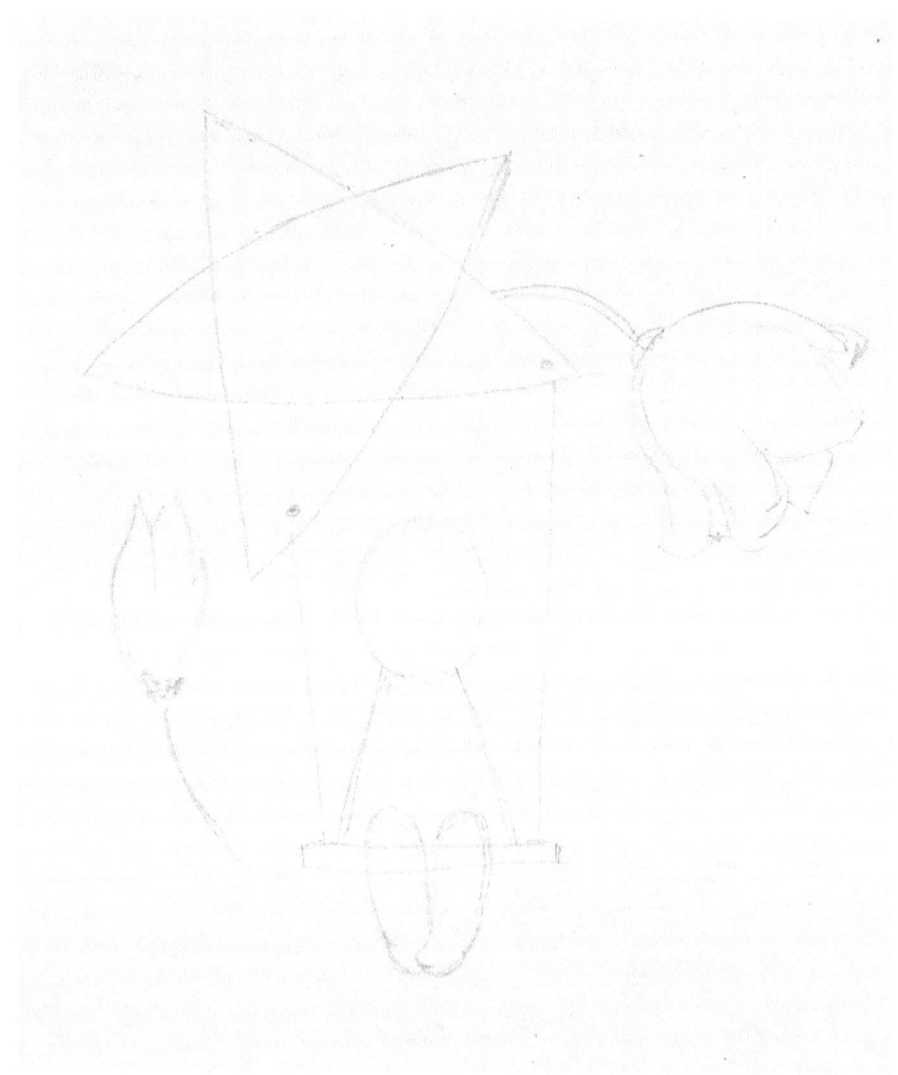

Step two, you are adding the boundaries of the girl's body as well as the flowers. These are big strokes and shapes. Check the curving lines and sweeping motions.

Step Three

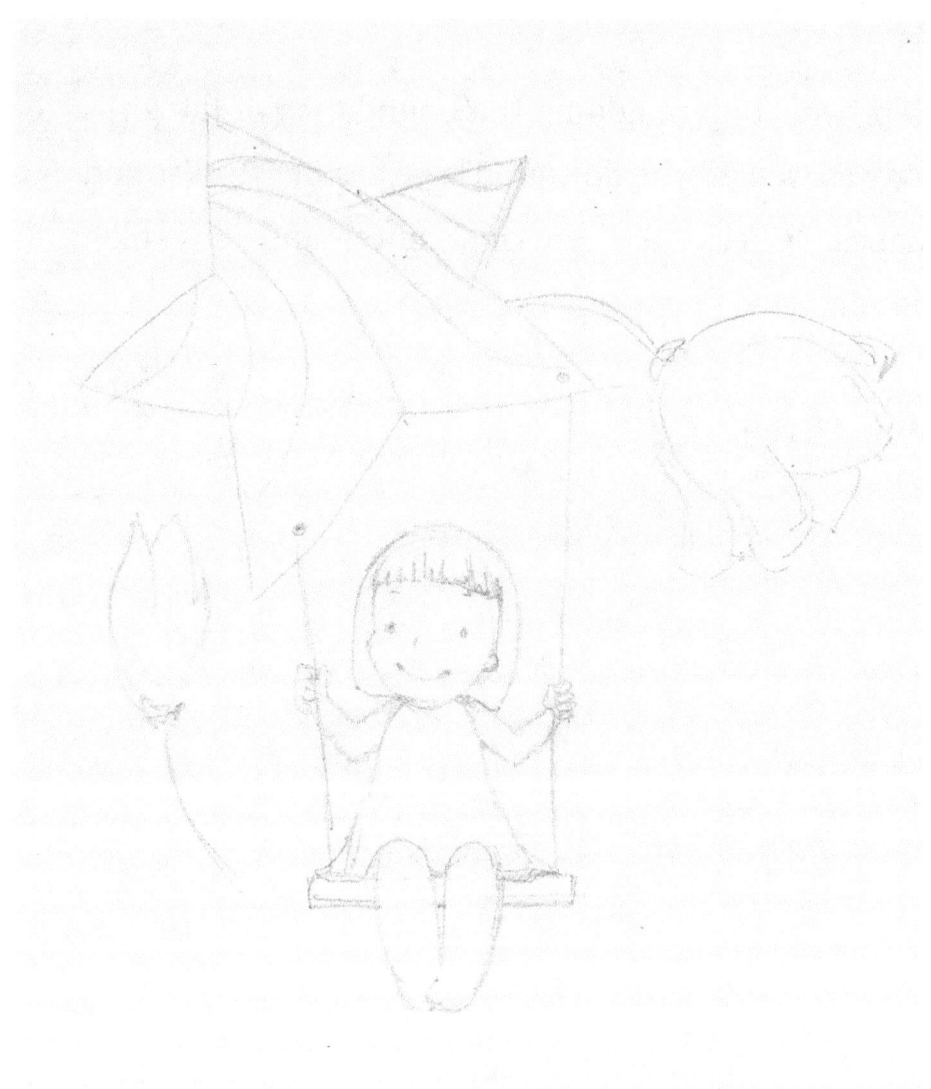

This step is for a little more detail in the facial features. They are usually subtle and light. These are no different.

Step Four

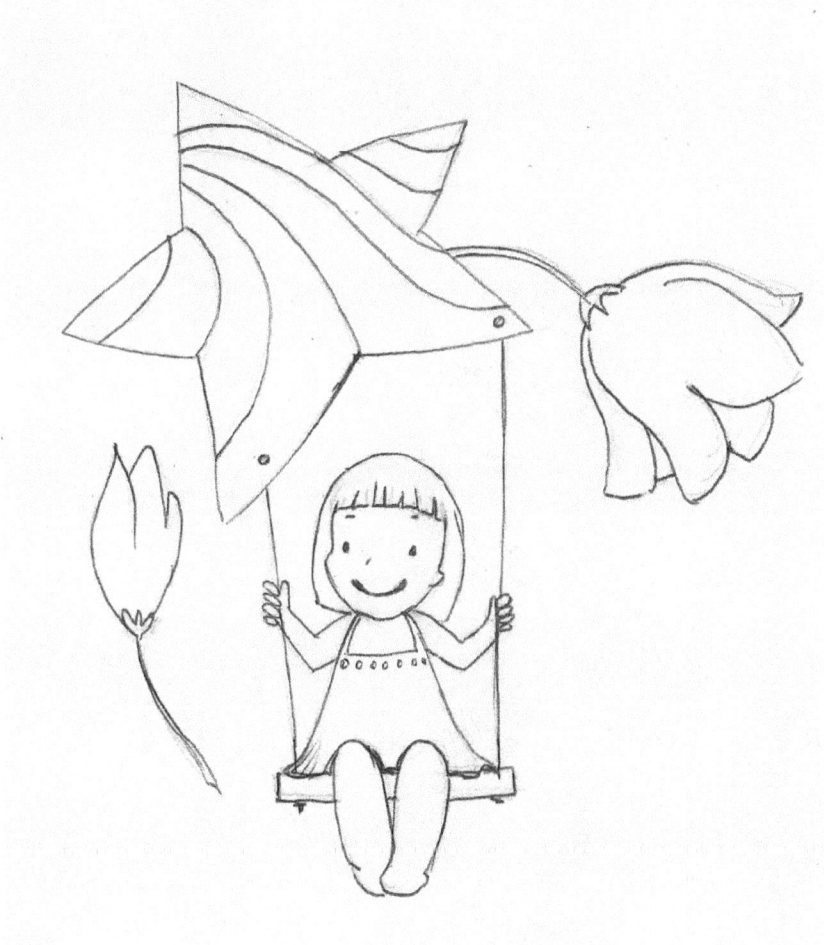

It is time for ink. You want to find your lines that make sense and erase the rest. You can always pen in the lines you want, allow them to dry, and then erase the excess pencil. Again, check your paper and the books drawing to make sure you have gotten all the lines and details in up to this point.

Step Five

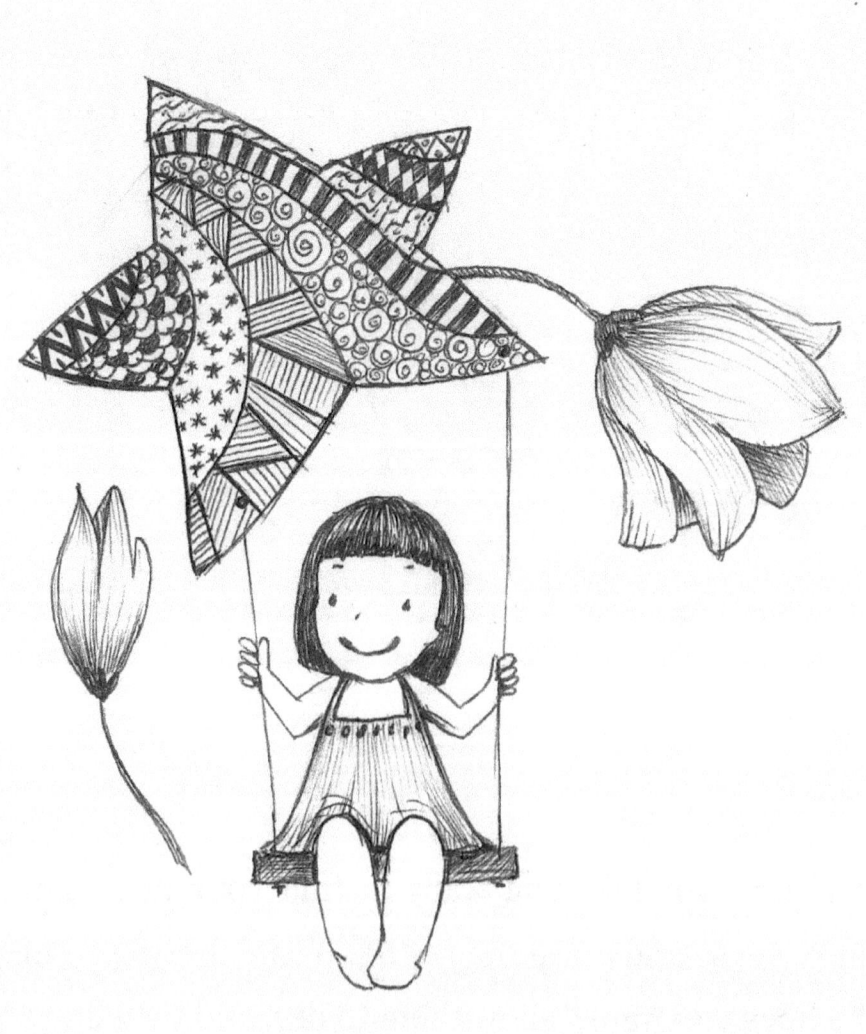

This final step is very much fun. You are drawing in the shapes and designs of the star, as well as the shades of the flowers and dress. You always want to set your boundaries in the large object before designing, and then enjoy the repetitious drawing of the pattern.

Chapter Eight - Rabbit and Heart

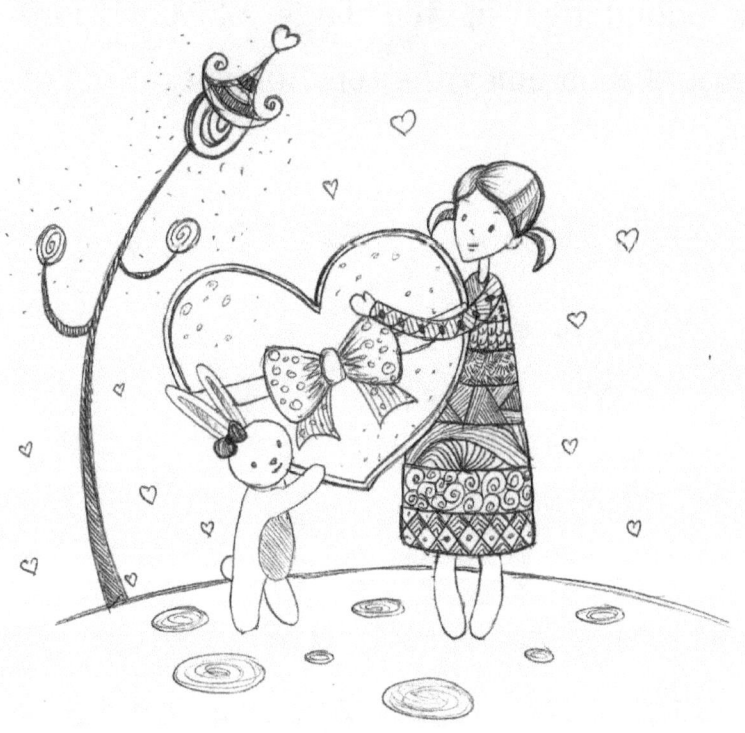

Step One

Step one, you will draw the heart's center a little left of the center of the page. Make the heart big, and then draw the figure. You see the curve of the legs and draw accordingly.

Step Two

Step two is about adding that big curved line on the bottom to create the hill, and the addition of the bunny is nice. Remember and notice the rounded chunky type of figures to create the cuteness.

Step 2

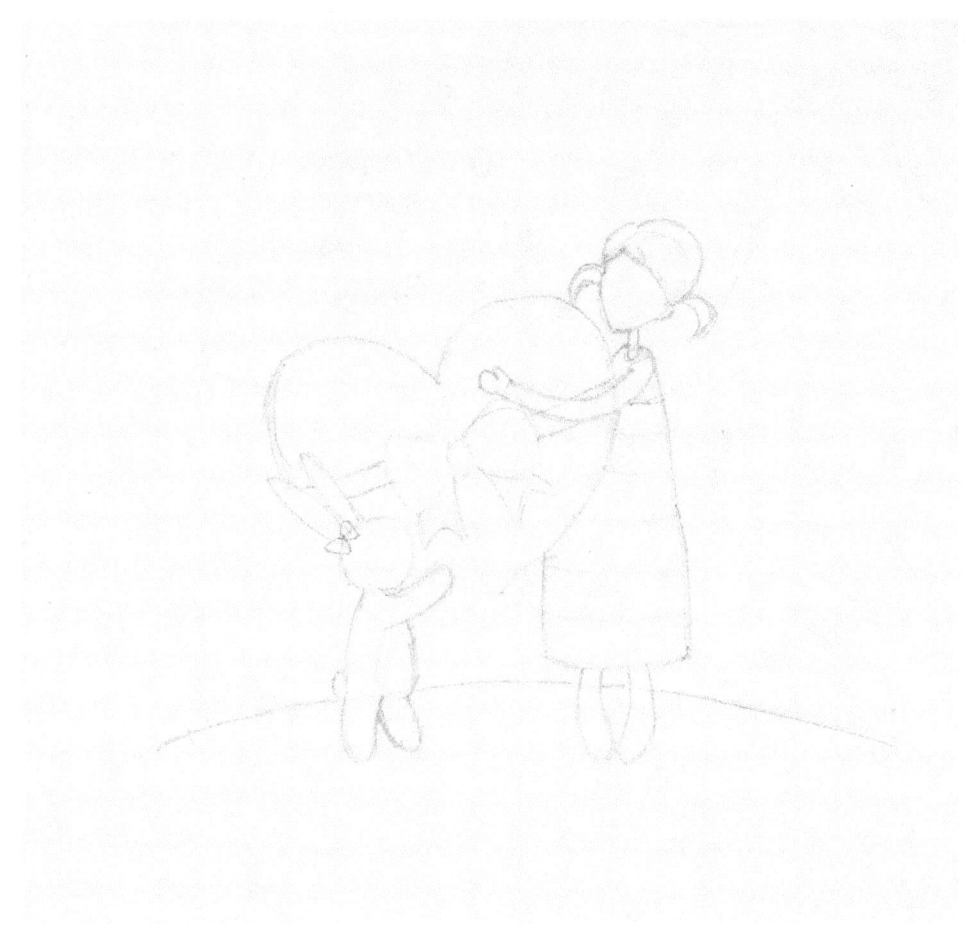

Step three is about small details. The hair on the girl
and the bow on the rabbit are made of two small
shapes. Compare and contrast your picture to this so
that everything looks right.

Step 4

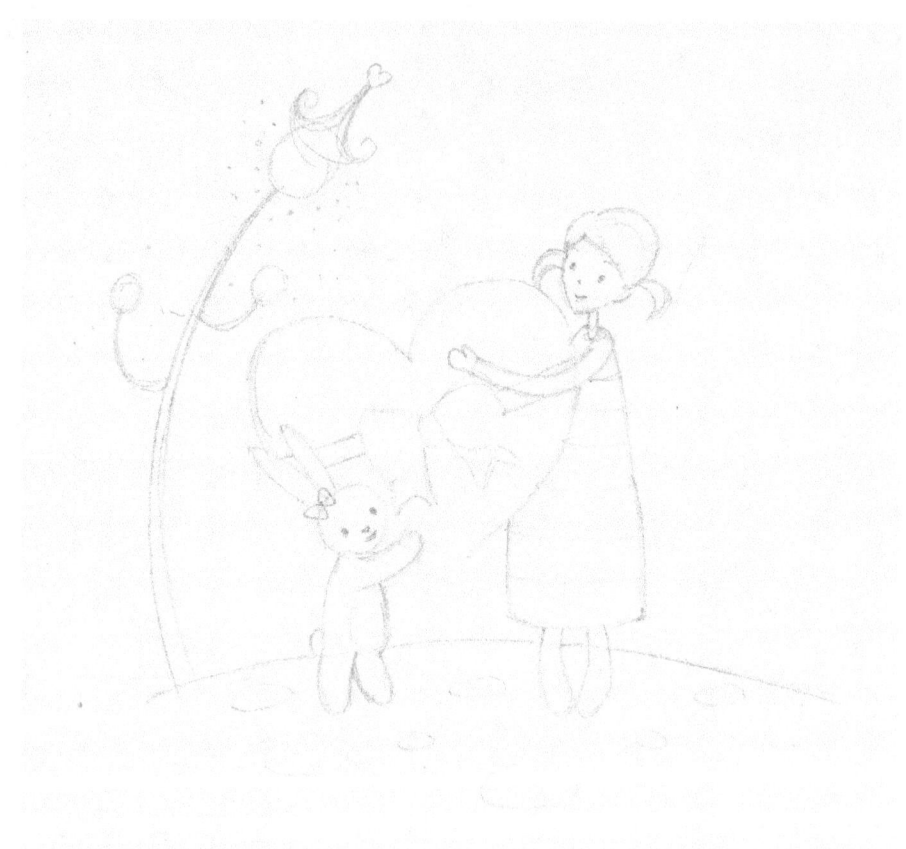

This is the step at which you add the light posts and a few circles on the ground for design. Make sure they are different sizes. You also will add little flecks everywhere for effect.

Step Four

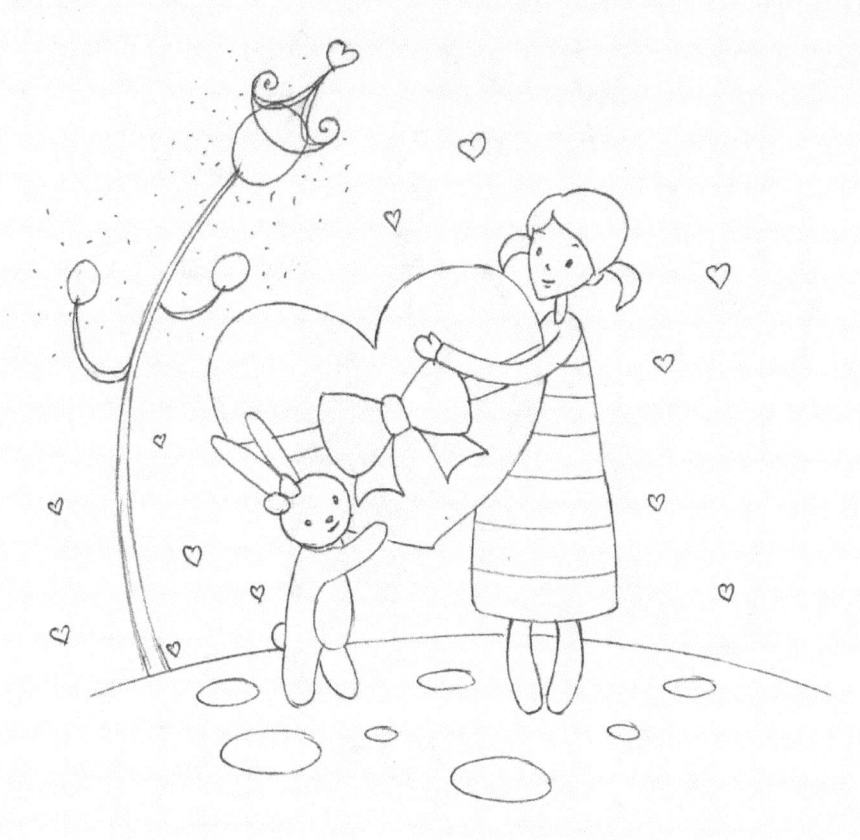

And now it is time for outline ink, and to erase all unwanted lines. Don't forget to turn those dots into hearts.

Step 5

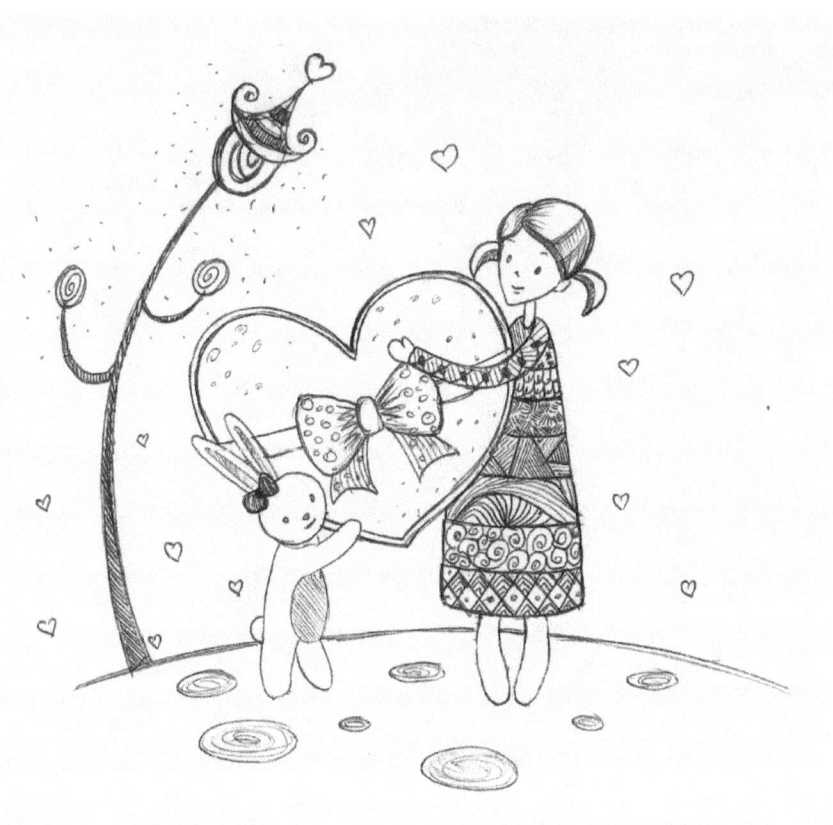

In this final step, enjoy yourself and design away with the swirls and straight lines. You will create the shade on the light posts with the hatch lines as well. Check back and forth so you have created your masterpiece to your liking, and fill in the circles a little for the nice effect.

Chapter Nine - Modern Woman

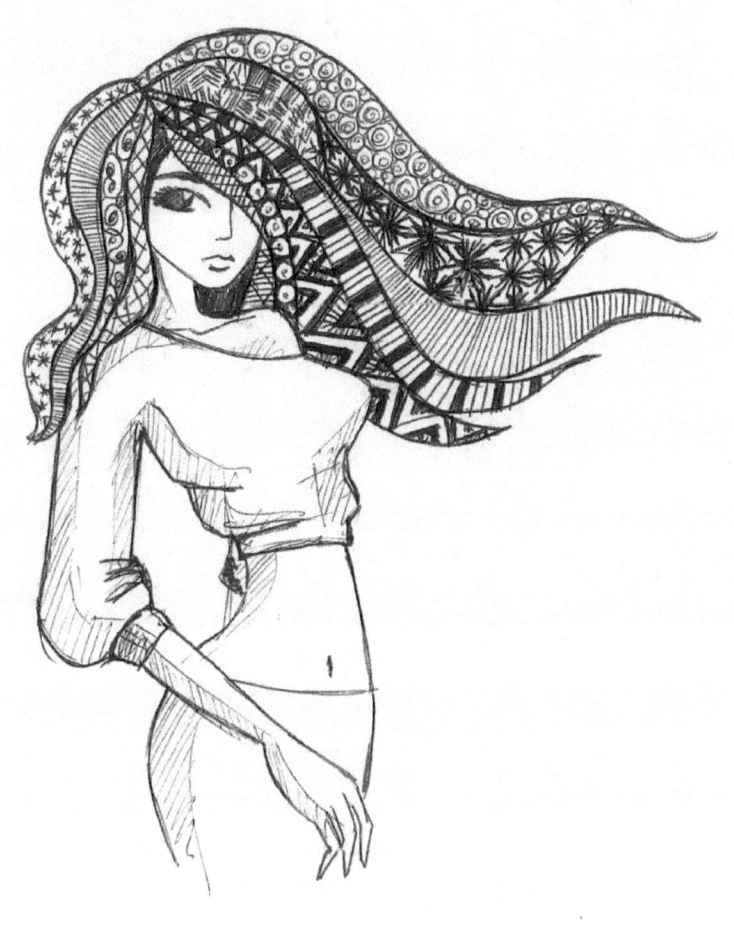

Step One

Step one, outline her body, noting her curves, and placing the figure slightly to the left of the center of the page.

Step Two

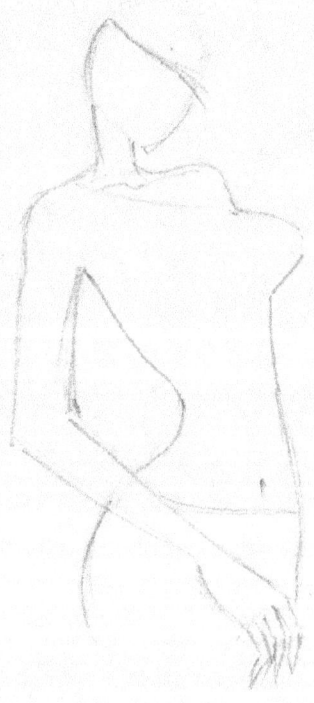

Step two, you want get the angle of her head and the extension of her breast, as well as her fingers.

Step Three

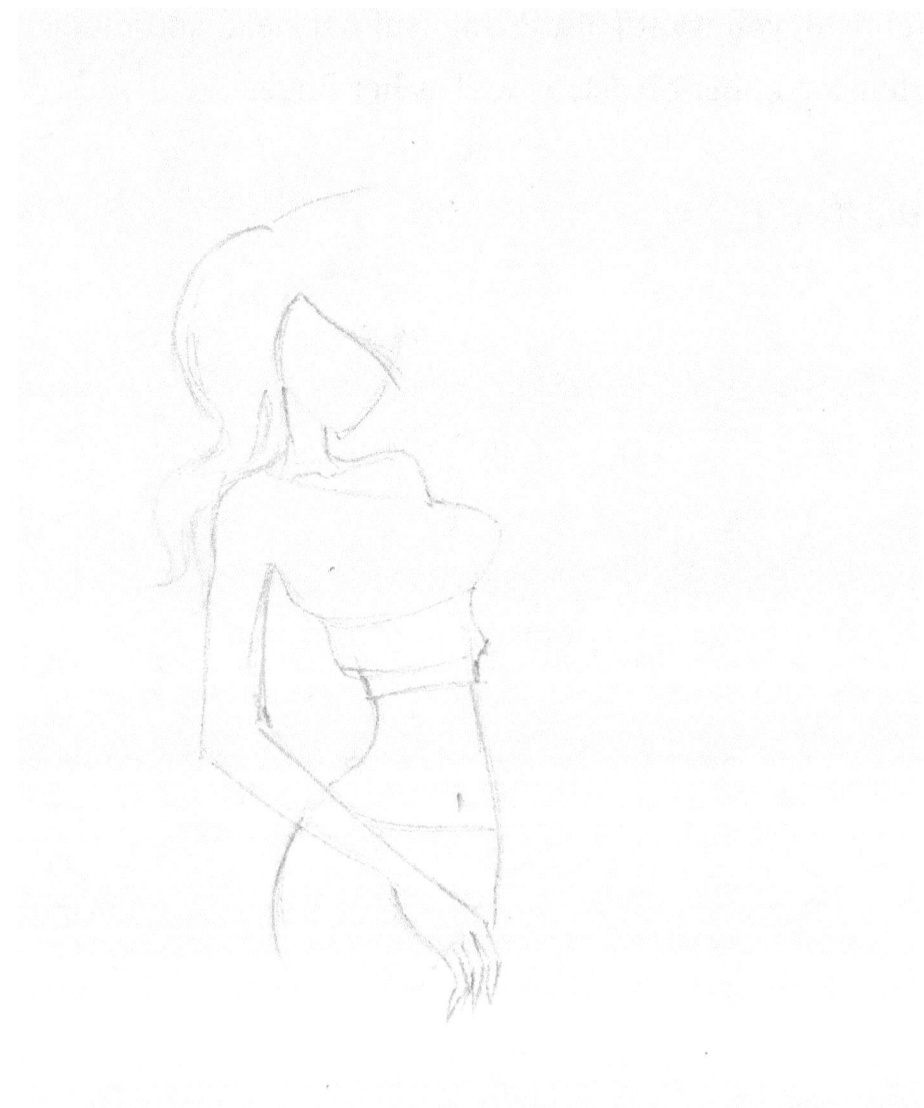

Step three, you are working on drawing more of her curves. You might have to erase some of the lines to get the angles correct. Note how far out her shoulder is from her waist.

Step Four

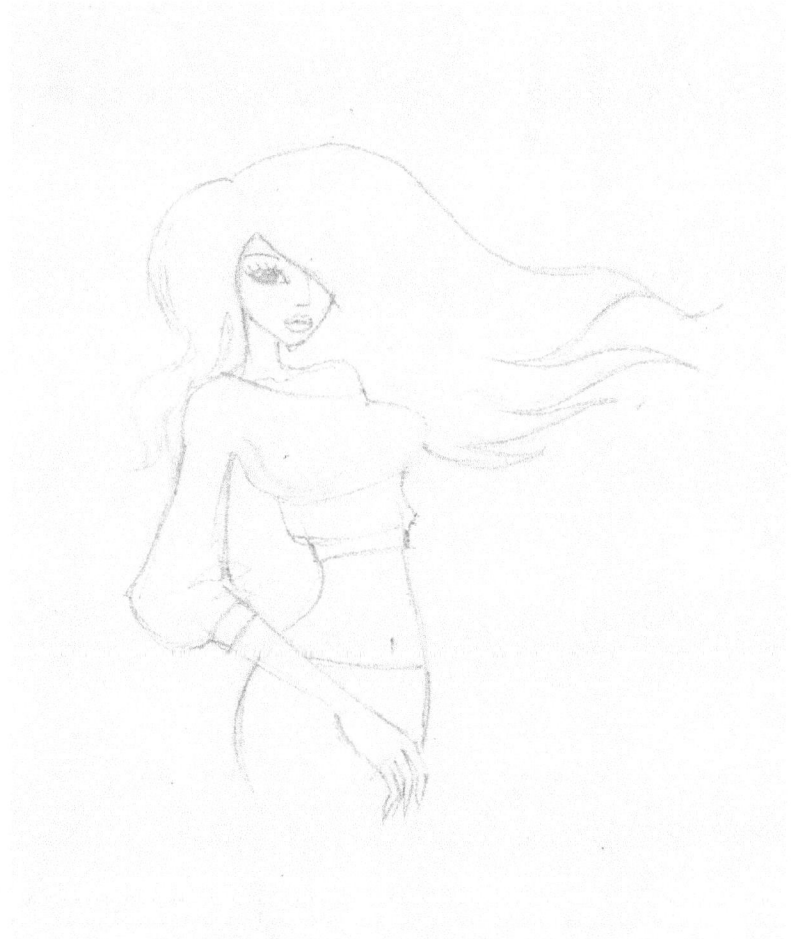

Step four is all about the hair, and extending it out from the page. You are using waving lines. It is also time for facial features.

Step Five

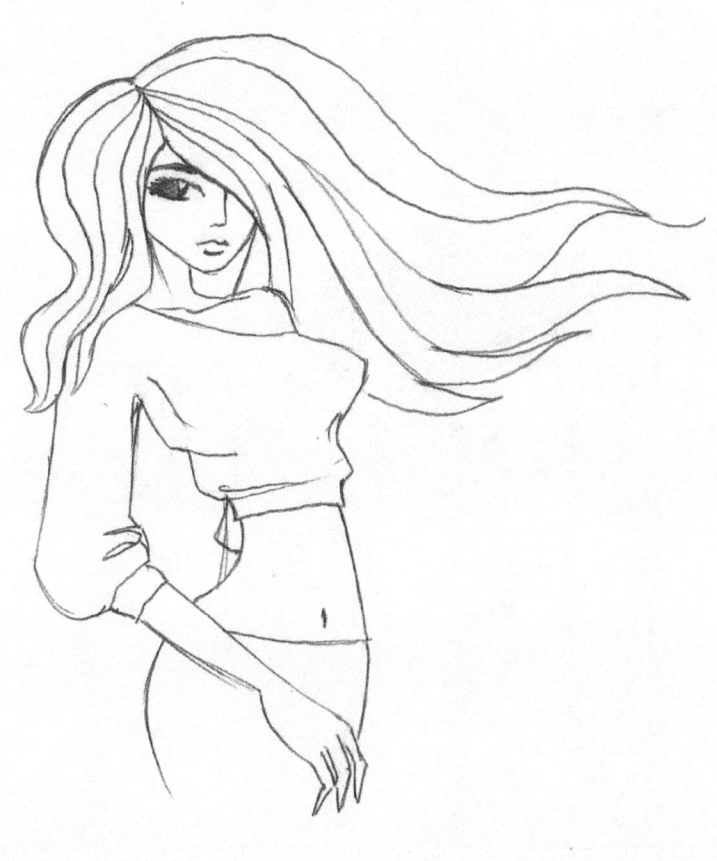

Step five is all about the ink. Once you feel confident that your pencil drawing has got all the right angles, then you can go ahead over the lines with a pen and help make the picture come to life.

Step Six

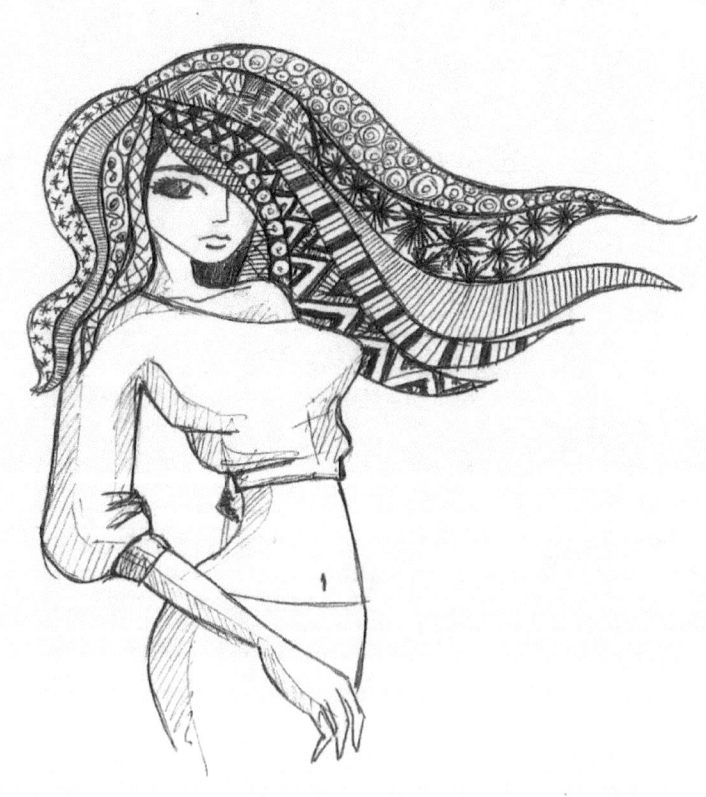

In this final step and final drawing, you will be adding the detail of the hair to complete this modern woman.

Make sure that you make your design partitions first so that you can design away within the boundaries of the line. You also will be doing loose wide hatching as well to create the light shade of the woman's body. Remember to always step back from your drawing to see how yours compares to the one on the book.

Conclusion

As you can see, there are very definite elements of amazing pictures that repeat themselves. The position of each main subject is not quite in the center. The main subject can be positioned in any one of the three sections of your paper, either placed in the horizontal position or vertical position. To make a picture interesting, you want a variation in the direction of the lines. You can see the lines of each picture go up or down in different degrees as a direction coming from the center of the page. These variations make the picture very pleasing and interesting to the eye.

If you will notice with the figures you have to have the body parts look strong enough for our eye to read the leg as a real leg. It has to look strong. When drawing different angles of the body, you want to be clear to create the shape that the body part makes up on the page, and not what you believe a body part to look like. A drawing is made up of shapes and lines.

Reality is our minds making sense of those shapes and lines. Our minds just think lines, but that is not really what your eye is seeing when you look at anything. Most lines are imperfect, and you have to draw things that way.

By this time, you can probably create your own small scenes using the techniques you have learned in this book. It is very exciting to go out and choose figures that you care about, and create them all your own. Remember that you can embellish your drawing with a little decoration and design with the circle and stripes as well as squares and diamonds.

You want to create clean lines by either having quick confident strokes, or build your lines by connecting small lines where when they come together they read as one line. Drawing requires a loose light hand and wrist to create the contrast. You want to watch the heavy hatching so that you do not darken your picture too much, because you cannot take too much dark pen away and it will not look right.

If your pictures do not look like these pictures at first, don't worry. You can erase and try again or you can start fresh. Just keep trying, and draw the lines as many times as you want. There is no timeline to learning drawing. You simply want to try until you get it. You don't have to worry about inking your drawing until you feel confident that your pencil drawing is looking close to what you see in the pictures in the book. When in doubt, just simply start from top to bottom and match all the lines you see in the picture with what you have on your paper. If you are concerned with your line not looking confident enough, then keep erasing until you get that swift fast confident line. Remember you want to draw with a nice loose wrist.

I hope you enjoyed learning to make amazing drawings and continue to do so. The most exciting thing is to continue with your art experience and to start creating drawings of your own. Show people your work, and inspire them to draw as well. Drawing is a wonderful way to funnel positive energy through your body and into the world. Drawing is a peaceful soothing hobby that will help you stay calm and uses other parts of your brain that you may otherwise not use. I thank you for reading, and hope you enjoyed drawing these amazing pictures.

www.ingramcontent.com/pod-product-compliance
Lightning Source LLC
Chambersburg PA
CBHW051342170526
45166CB00002B/913